The Optimist Dinghy
1947-2007

A provisional history of the first sixty years of
the International Optimist dinghy

Robert Wilkes
with Clifford McKay Jr.

The Optimist Dinghy 1947-2007
A Provisional History of the
First Sixty Years of the
International Optimist Dinghy

ISBN 978-1484911969

Published in 2013 by Robert Wilkes (robert@wilkessail.net)

Clark Mills
1915-2001

"A boat, by God, its just a gleamin' beautiful creation. And when you pull the sail up on a boat, you've got a little bit of really somethin' God-given. Man, it goes bleetin' off like a bird wing, you know, and there's nothin' else like it."

Clark Mills

Preface

This little book should perhaps more accurately be called a chronicle. I have been personally involved in the events described for the last thirty-odd years and have had the privilege of knowing almost all the most influential people of the earlier period, with the much regretted exception of Clark Mills himself.

It is moreover largely a chronicle of IODA, the International Optimist Dinghy Association. The Optimist is used for many activities but the requirement of ISAF, the International Sailing Federation, is that IODA offers "a high standard of international competitive sailing". This book is devoted almost entirely to the efforts of IODA to do just that.

This edition is provisional. The information to hand is limited, in particular for the 1960s and 1970s, and additional information, as well as any corrections, would be appreciated. With digital printing it is viable to produce a second, more inclusive edition. I am grateful to Cliff McKay, the first boy to sail an Optimist dinghy, for his carefully researched study of the earliest days. It is summarised in chapter one but he has kindly agreed to include a fuller account as a supplement.

As a chronicle it attempts to report facts and figures. Motives and opinions are, wherever possible, supported by quotations from the time. Statistics have acquired a bad name but, as a retired businessman, I depended on numeric data and the statistics I use are, to the best of my ability, accurate and meaningful.

Like most chroniclers, I am biased. However I was trained as a historian and declare my bias. Just as Bede assumed that christianity was a good thing, I assume that sport is about educating young people through competitive activity. I also assume - perhaps naively - that the Olympics should "inspire a generation" so you will find many references to the later Olympic achievements of the young sailors. I rather regret that it has been easier to trace future Olympians than those who achieved success in other areas of sailing or indeed outside of our sport.

Any opinions expressed are mine alone and are not necessarily those of IODA or anyone else.

I cannot claim to be objective about Helen Mary. I record her contribution to the history of the Optimist and I do not believe I have over-estimated it.

Finally I apologise to those who may find this chronicle boring. "We had joy, we had fun, we had seasons in the sun", but I leave it to someone else to record that.

Robert Wilkes
Howth, June 2013

Notes:

1. Sources: I have tried to list the main external sources and apologise where I have failed to do so. Omissions will be corrected in the next edition on request.

2. Pictures: in most cases I have been unable to establish the origin. More recently I acknowledge the work of Tim Wilkes (no relation). Omissions will be corrected in the next edition on request.

3. People: Very many individuals have contributed to the progress of the Optimist. With the greatest regret I decided that it was too difficult to mention some without offending others. Therefore in general I name only members of the IODA Executive and occasionally other committees. An exception is made for the early pioneers who introduced the boat in certain countries.

4. Names: in most cases I have used the name of the sailor as it appears on score-sheets or articles of the time. For IODA officers I have tended to use their full name when it first occurs but their first name only thereafter.
   For place names I have used what I regard as the most recognisable form. Countries are given their English names. Great Britain is used instead of the United Kingdom because Northern Irish Optimists are normally registered with the Irish Sailing Association.

5. Language: my use of English may seem formal to native speakers but I have always found it easier to read foreign languages when written formally rather than in journalese. I notice that translation engines such as Google feel the same. American spelling is used in direct American quotations.

6. Punctuation: I have used commas etc. more widely than is usual. I find them useful when reading foreign languages and hope they may help non-Anglophone readers. I apologise for the lack of some accents, particularly in Slav names.

Thanks

I acknowledge with thanks the input of Nigel Ringrose, Al Chandler, Michel Barbier, Fred Kats and Curly Morris.

The Author

- born and educated in England at Downside; graduated in history from Jesus College, Cambridge. Moved to Ireland in 1969.
- has played very many sports, specialising in fencing and (field) hockey. From 1976-1986 he was a member of the Commission des Statuts of the Fédération Internationale d'Escrime
- took up sailing when his sons were in Optimists. A member of Howth Y.C, he raced a Squib (19' keelboat) and chartered in Europe and the Caribbean
- secretary of IODA 1997-2007
- married since 1966 to Helen Mary, q.v.
- two sons; both represented Ireland at the Optimist Worlds. One has sailed five Fastnets and a Sydney-Hobart, and manufactures carbon-fibre spars. Two grandsons: one is beginning to sail an Optimist . . .

Contents

Chapter

1	A legend is born: 1947-1953	5
2.	Europe and beyond 1954-1970	13
3	The 1970s	25
4	The 1980s	33
5	The 1990s	48
6	The 'IOD95' Project	67
7	The World Championship Debate	73
8	2000-2007	76
9	Girls	94
10	Training & Development	99
11	How many Optimists?	101
12	The Optimist and the Olympics	104
13	Summary - the Optimist in 2007	106

Appendix: Executive Committee Members 1962-2007   110

Supplement by Cliff McKay Jr.

Chapter

i	The Origin of the Optimist Pram	113
ii	"I sailed the first Optimist pram"	118
iii	Program Rules & Regulations	123
iv	Clarke Mills, the Designer of the Optimist Pram	129

Chapter 1: A legend is born: 1947-1953

There are many versions of the story of the birth of the Optimist. The following is based on the account of Clifford McKay Jr., the first boy to sail Clark Mills' prototype, with input from an interview with Clark himself by Bill Douglas when editor of the USODA *Optinews*.

In 1947 the Clearwater Optimist Club, which had been formed that spring, sponsored a 'Soapbox Derby'. This was raced down the only hill in Clearwater in carts designed, built (from materials sponsored by club members) and driven by boys, among them Cliff. The road then reverted to normal use and that was it.

To Cliff's father Major McKay this once-off event was frustrating. In mid-August he was invited to speak to the Optimist Club and proposed a number of possible ongoing projects. Cliff Junior, then aged 12, had already sailed with the local Snipe fleet so one of the projects was a weekly 'Orange Crate Derby' using boats rather than carts and taking advantage of the freely available waters of the shallow lagoon of Clearwater Bay. This was the project which captured the imagination of the members and Major McKay was asked to investigate.

The following day he contacted Clark Mills, proud owner of the Clark Mills Boat Works. His brief was to design a sailboat that could be constructed for $50 and use a bedsheet for a sail - though Clark rapidly talked him out of the latter idea. Within two weeks Clark built a prototype, painted it red, brought it to the Haven Street dock and took it for a sail. Then, to quote Cliff Junior: *"he turned it over to me. It was lively and accelerated smartly as the sail filled. It turned sharply when I put the tiller over. The bow didn't dig in. It lifted and the boat seemed to skip across the water. The low sprit rig and generous beam gave it good stability. It was fun and easy to sail. I thought: 'Wow, this is neat'."*

The boat was displayed the next Thursday at the Optimist Club Meeting. The members were delighted. They formed an Optimist Pram Committee, members being W. Watson, Art Lee, Ben Magrew and Maynard Barney. Within a week Major McKay and this newly formed committee had secured sponsors to cover the costs of 28 boats, and Clark Mills was put to work building them.

The people:

Clark Mills

Clark was the grandson of a cabinet maker and his family moved to Florida when he was three. Even in his teens he had built sailing dinghies and with friends founded the Clearwater Junior Yacht Club at the Haven Street Dock. During the war he worked at the Philadelphia Navy Yard and was later based in the Panama Canal Zone, building sailboats in his spare time.
Returning to Clearwater after the war he established the Clark Mills Boat Works. As he himself put it: "I had this shop and these machines but I didn't have no d*m*ed orders". Clark was a delightfully outspoken individualist with no false modesty. *"I think I'm the best designer in the United States. I'm damn good. I've got the splinters and the backache to prove it."*

Major Clifford A. McKay

Major McKay had served in France during the war and had received the *croix de guerre* for "exceptional services during the liberation of France". A newspaper reporter by training, on his return he established the McKay Advertising Agency. He never was a sailor, preferring to be on the water fishing, but had seen the pleasure his son had taken in sailing a Snipe. His big concern was to involve young people in constructive activities. He was described by Clark as "a mover and a shaker and a shouter. He was a Rotary Club man and a good speaker. He spent many hours promoting the prams in Service Clubs, Optimist, Lions, Rotary and Kiwanis, and in Yacht Clubs around Florida."

The Clearwater Optimist Club

McKay was not a member of the Optimist Club so the leading member of the Optimist Pram Committee was Ben Magrew. Specialist sailing knowledge was provided by Guy Roberts and Wallis Skinner from the Clearwater Yacht Club Snipe Fleet. The following year the Committee was joined by Ernie Green, owner of Green's Moving and Storage. Contrary to some reports he was not one of the original promoters of the programme but he used his van to transport boats to regattas, especially when the Optimist was included in Florida Sailing Association races. One memory is that "the huge green van towered over the cars and trailers at the launch site. The back doors opened and out came a steady stream of small boats and small sailors."

The boat

In an interview with Bill Douglas, then editor of USODA *Optinews*, Clark clarified his thoughts on the design. The length of the boat was dictated by the standard length of sheets of plywood, with 8 foot sheets (nominally 2440mm) being the most economical. Within that length there was no way to bend the wood to a sharp bow. In fact, though no one is accusing Clark of plagiarism, other 8 foot

blunt-ended dinghies already existed such as the MacGregor Sabot and its derivatives, and the Hagerty Sea Shell which was used for a time at the St. Petersburg Y.C.

Clark built a jig to hold the transom, the bow, and a mid-ship thwart. He joined them together with narrow cypress stringers. He glued and nailed quarter-inch plywood over the frame. Clark said: "I hammered it together in a day and a half with ridged nails, slapped on a coat of paint and called her an Optimist Pram."

The frame on which the pram was built. Re-using the frame made commercial building more economical and more one-design.

As a boat designer Clark was not perhaps quite the 'simple man' he claimed to be. He is on record as a builder of very fast versions of the Snipe, at the time probably the largest dinghy class in the world. This may have led him to give his new little pram a 'rocker' (shape of the bottom of the hull) precisely raised at the bow to keep the stubby bow out of the water. As Cliff put it after his first sail: "The bow didn't dig in".

A few modifications to the earliest boats were needed. Cliff recalls:

"At first the sheet ran from the boom, through a block on the top of the tiller. You could hold the tiller and sheet in one hand. There was no cleat, no traveler. These came later. When you mounted the rudder fittings on the boat and on the rudder, you had to make sure to get it right or the sheet would lift the rudder up and off. This mistake produced some exciting moments as the boat sailed off with no means to steer it."

Comparing the first known drawing of the Clearwater Optimist with the earlier photo of 'P6' shows that a traveller has been introduced and a primitive boom down-haul - scarcely worthy of the name vang - has been added. The horizontal 'bench', reportedly around 4"/100mm wide, at the centre thwart has been abandoned, making it easier for the sailor to move along the hull. The diagonal for-

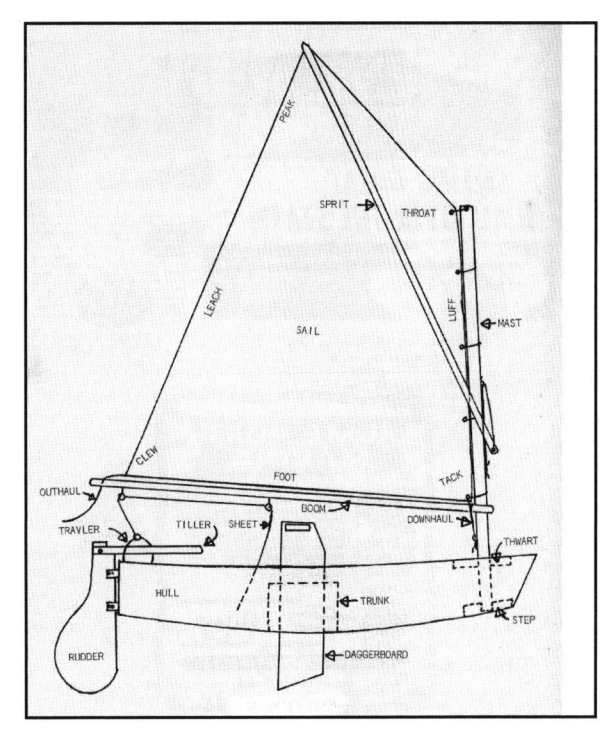

ward edge of the daggerboard is reported as a means to keep the board in place but it is clear from other photos that it was also used to rake the board aft and there was considerable variation on the shape of the diagonal.

Another notable feature of the photo of 'P6' is the lack of buoyancy, either in the boat or on the sailor. This is confirmed by other early photos. Cliff is emphatic that additional buoyancy was felt to be unnecessary since the wooden Optimist was itself sufficiently buoyant. It is interesting that there is no buoyancy visible on the early Optimists shown in the Danish museum in Svendborg or the first (Danish) Optimist imported into England. However the need for *personal* buoyancy was soon appreciated and it is recorded that shortly afterwards sailors had to provide their own life jackets or (water) ski belts.

The mast was a 1.5/8" (41.3mm) curtain pole and the boom and sprit made of square-section timber, 1" (25.4mm) and 3/4" (19mm) respectively.

The una-spritsail gave adjustable belly to the sail run up by local sailmaker Dickie Moore and his wife - of cotton duck of course; Dacron was not used in sailing until 1954. These early sails consisted of three panels with *vertical* seams. A bolt rope of 1/4" (6mm) hemp extended from the peak, along the luff and foot of the sail and formed the outhaul to the end of the boom, but the sail was loose footed.

The original idea had been that the boats would be built, as were the Soapbox Derby carts, by the boys but Cliff writes that, contrary to popular myth:

> *"We boys never built the hull. Even Clark's straight-forward design wasn't easy for amateur builders. I know, I built four later with my son. Clark produced the basic hull and we boys took it from there, fastening the corner caps, installing the bow thwart and mast step, scraping off the glue that dripped down, sanding, painting, shaping the rudder and daggerboard edges, bending the rudder fittings from galvanized sheet metal in the vice at the school woodworking shop, and tying the sail to the mast with venetian blind cord from the hardware store."*

The Organisation

Major McKay and the Optimist Club applied the sponsorship concept of the Soap Box Derby to the new boats. Each would be owned by a local merchant and would carry his advertising on the sides of the hull which was not only allowed but recommended. Indeed some of the earliest newspaper reports read as if regatta results were those of the sponsors rather than the skippers, for example: *"Prams of the Clearwater Sun and radio station WTAN . . . tied for points."*

It was a condition of the sponsorship that the selected skippers participated in weekly Sunday afternoon races. The founding fathers were quite explicit:

> *"Racing, rather than just day-sailing, is emphasized in the Pram program. Experience has shown that this provides the most interest for the skippers and that the character building aspects are better realized when competition is involved. The organization which governs racing in the class is known as the OPTIMIST CLASS PRAM INTERNATIONAL RACING ASSOCIATION."*

But the young sailors were allowed to do as they wished with their boats at other times of the week. Cliff recalls that:

> *"After school and on Saturdays, we'd launch our boats and explore Clearwater Bay and its mangrove islands on our own. The only rule was "Do not sail in the Gulf". We'd help each other carry the boats to the water and to make sail. Of course when two or more boats sail together, it's a race." "I discovered that my pram would stand up nicely in 30 knots, the only problem was bailing out the spray that splashed in."*

The other rule was that Optimists were only allowed to sail together with another Optimist or other boat but that seems to have been the limit on safety procedure.

The three-panel vertical-cut sail. It cannot have been easy to set

By 1950 some sails were coloured

The Optimist Club logo, stencilled on from 1948, was added to the earlier . club letters such as 'C' (for Clearwater) as above.

Advertising by sponsors was *recommended.*

Within a year the Optimist had spread to nearby fleets in Dunedin, Pass-a-Grille, and St. Petersburg, and in December 1948 an 'International Pram Regatta' was held. A fire the following year destroyed 29 of the Clearwater fleet but this actually proved positive publicity and sponsors were found for no less than 43 new Optimists.

Over-all Clark is reported to have built around 200 prams in the period but the Optimist Club also sold the plans at $5 for anyone to build. In 1955 the plans were even printed in the magazine *Woman's Day* for all to read. An Optimist Class Pram International Racing Association was formed and by 1968 there were more than twenty fleets all over Florida, most of them hosting at least one annual regatta. The two biggest were the International, held in March in Clearwater and so called from as early as 1950, and the Florida State Pram Championship which alternated from an East Coast host fleet to a West Coast host fleet each year.

In summary as again recorded by Cliff:

"The beginnings of the Optimist Pram were a labor of love. Dad conceived a unique plan so all kids could have a chance to sail. He then promoted the pram all around the State of Florida. Clark Mills' creativity designed this lively little boat, built most of the first hulls, and donated the copyright to the Clearwater Optimist Club. The Club spent countless hours with the program, supervising races, working with the boys and girls, and transporting them to regattas. No one received royalties or any remuneration. They did it so boys and girls could have fun sailing, and grow up as better citizens."

Later development

But for the next three decades the future of Clark Mills' brilliant design as an international class did not lie in the USA. By 1953 it was reported that there were pram fleets in ten states as well as Canada and Cuba, but the Clearwater plans included tolerances and options so wide that any sense of a one-design suitable for racing was lost. One Dunedin sailor recalls that in the 1960s: "Some prams were better equipped than others and we 'owned' certain ones. Some 50% of the fleet were the older original wooden ones which none of us wanted. Now they're in museums". Even into the 1980s in Florida there were *two* Optimists, the 'IODA Pram' and the 'Clearwater Optimist Pram', sailing as separate Classes in the same regattas; indeed the same family might own both types.

In 1964 the American team at the 'Worlds' in Århus got a chance to see the changes made by the Danes and in 1966 Florida hosted the event. Among the USA team in 1972 in Sweden was the great Ed Baird who, along with Allison Jolly, the first ever female Olympic gold medallist, had been prize-winners at the national pram championship.

The USA supported the 1970 application to the IYRU, but as late as 1980 the USODA reported that the number of registered Optimists was less than 300. Of the registered Optimists 80 had been imported within the previous year. These included 20 bought by David Sinclair of the Noroton Y.C. in Darien, Connecticut due to the influence of Nigel Ringrose then stationed in the USA.

Chesapeake 1967: sails were now lateral

Sources:

The main source is Cliff McKay Jr. based on:

- an interview in April 2012 and subsequent correspondence
- articles published by him in *Southwinds* magazine in October 2011 through May 2012,
- an article by Eric Vibart published in *Voiles et Voiliers* in September 2007 and correspondence between McKay and Vibart
- extensive source material and correspondence supplied by McKay.

Additional information on Clark Mills is mainly based on a video interview with him by Bill Douglas http://www.youtube.com/watch?v=1IN5ULXEdUM and an article by Douglas *Simple Man, Simple Boat* published in USODA *Optinews* in 2003.

Additional sources include:

- The *Constitution & Bye-Laws of the Optimist Class Pram* (1948).
- The *Optimist Class Plan* (1973 edition) published by the Optimist Club of Clearwater
- *Twenty Years with the Clearwater Optimist Club Pram Fleet 1948-1968* published by the Optimist Club of Clearwater
- *Clark Mills' Boat Designs for the West Coast of Florida* by Tom Mayers
- *Clark Mills*, autobiographical notes edited by Daniel Mills
- Numerous articles in Florida newspapers of the period, including:
  - An article in the *Bradenton Times* May 2010 by Merab-Michal Favorite
  - Report in the *Palm Beach Post*, 13 March 1978
  - Articles by Anne McKay Garris (Cliff's sister) in the *Clearwater Gazette* and elsewhere
- Website of St. Petersburg Y.C.
- Hagerty Sea Shell: http://www.cohassetcolonials.com/cohasset-colonials-resources/about-cohasset-colonials/hagerty-sea-shell-boat.pdf
- MacGregor Sabot: http://en.wikipedia.org/wiki/Sabot_(dinghy)
- The Wooden Optimist Blog (http://woodenoptimist.blogspot.ie/p/opti-past.html) (Suffers from the usual defects of blogs)

Chapter 2: Europe and beyond: 1954-1970

The immediate future of Clark's design lay in Europe.

In 1954 Danish architect Axel Damgaard [sic] Olsen learned about the design. Unfortunately there is no evidence for the romantic idea that he imported one from Florida on a tall ship. As recorded by his great friend Gerald Elfendahl, he saw the Optimist in Clearwater while working on a freighter. It is also a myth that he saw the plans in *Woman's Day*. That publication was in June 1955 *after* the first Danish boats were built. Axel, who lived in Seattle from the late 1950s, was also the inspiration behind the International OK Dinghy.

Whatever the truth of these stories it probably was Axel who had the first seven built by Hans Christian Brorsen, dinghy chairman of the Sejlklubben Snekken and owner of a woodworking company. History relates that the first race was held on 15 April 1955 in Vordingborg.

The idea was taken up by Poul Gustav (P.G.) Hansen, a school-inspector from Hvidovre who is quoted as saying that building Optimists was better for his pupils than breaking open cigarette machines! Kits were available from Brorsen and it is recorded that more than 2,500 were sold over the next seven years, including exports.

In the following year Hansen and his great friend Viggo Jacobsen from Århus set up a 'self-selected committee within the Danish Yachting Association' (for ten years separate from its youth section) to promote the new boat. Bent Lyman's account of the period summarises that Hansen was the 'Interior Minister' and Viggo the 'Foreign Minister' of the partnership. Supported by the great Paul Elvstrøm, already winner of three Olympic golds, the idea spread throughout the country and by 1960 there were over 2,000 Optimists in 44 clubs in Denmark. A national championship (initially called a schools' championship) was created in 1957: the first winner, Ib Ussing Andersen, was to become CEO of North Sails Europe and as of 2006 tactician on a 94ft Wally Class yacht.

P.G. Hansen published in 1968 the 'how to rig and sail it' book *Optimistjollen: teknik, regler, taktik*. It was translated into English (as *First Steps in Small Boat Sailing* published in 1970 by Adlard Coles), French, German and Spanish and served as a brilliant guide to the strange new rig.

The Optimist was introduced to Finn Ryghelmer of the Royal Norwegian Y.C. who also started building. A Nordic Championship was established in 1959, the first edition being in Copenhagen. Sweden started to participate the following year with the first Optimists probably being sailed in the town of Viken, just across the Kattegat from Denmark, under the auspices of Carl Quiding. In Finland the first Optimist was imported from Denmark to Turku by Yrjö Valli in 1958: sadly he died in 1969 but by then Turku alone had 260 boats and his son Olavi continued with the Class for twenty years.

P.G. Hansen og Bent Aarre

Optimistjollen

J. FR. CLAUSENS FORLAG

The Danish plans of 1954
(Courtesy of the Danmarks Museum for Lystsejlads, Svendborg)

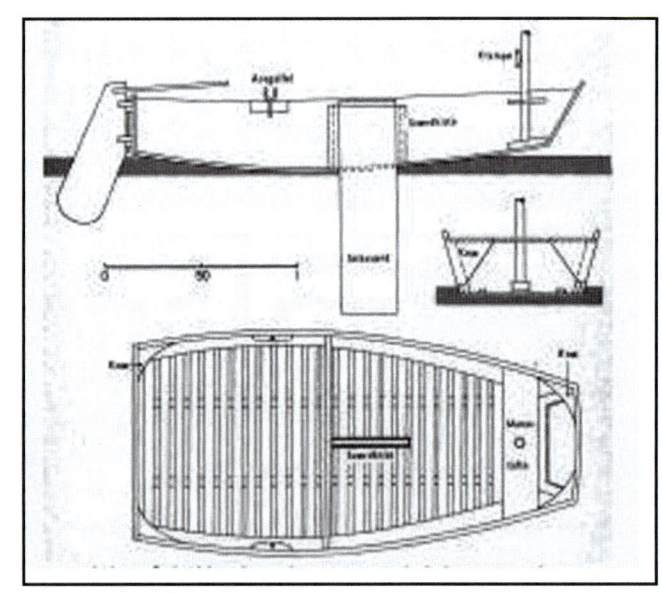

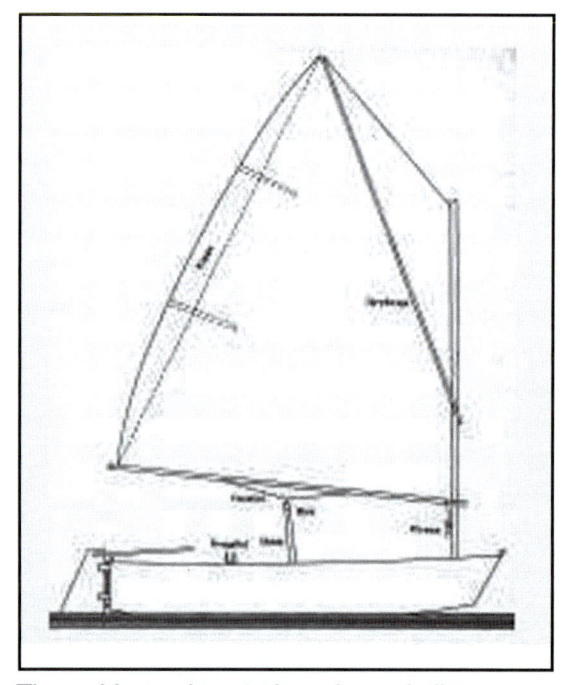

The lateral slats on the floor. This is confirmed by the earliest boat in the German museum in Esgrus but they may have been removable for racing.

The rudder and centreboard are similar to later designs and unlike the early prams. The transom sheeting of the Clearwater Pram has been moved to the centre of the boom. The strop from the boom to the mainsheet block looks very modern but see the cover of Hansen's book for a more traditional system. Sails are now made of lateral panels, are fitted with two battens and extend beyond the peak-to-clew line.

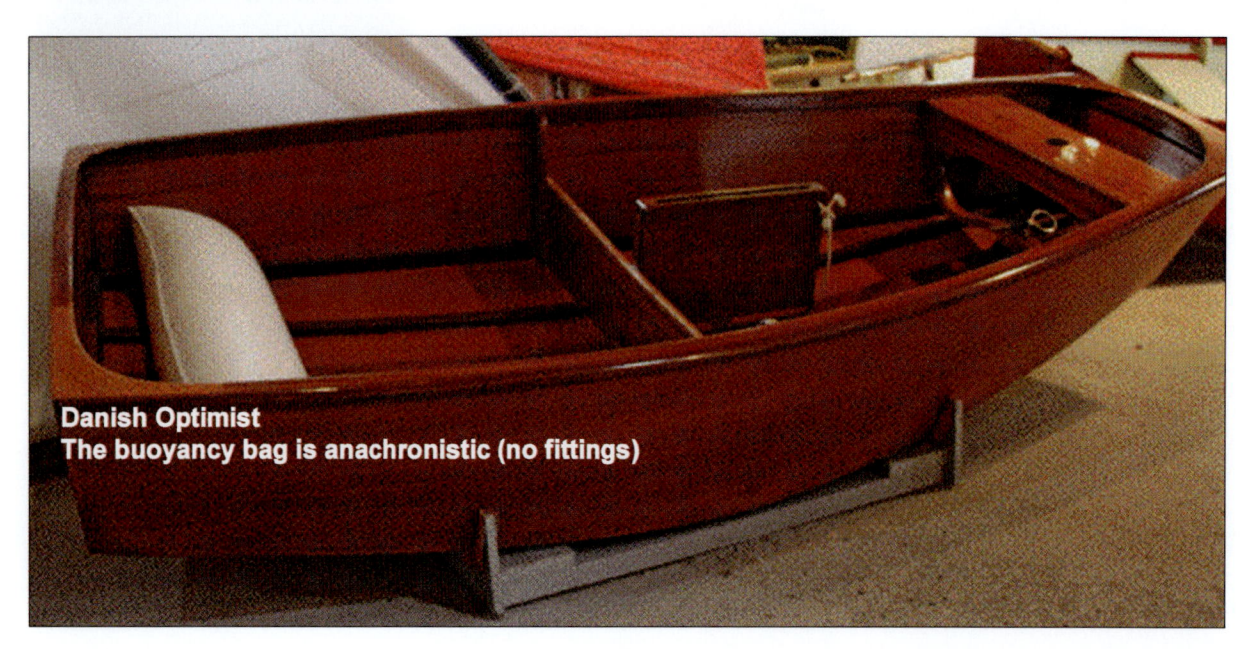

Danish Optimist
The buoyancy bag is anachronistic (no fittings)

Technical changes

As the Clearwater pram of 1947 metamorphosed into the International Optimist of the 1973 rules, it is sometimes hard to know when changes occurred, not least because the specification of the Clearwater pram itself changed over the period. Moreover at the foundation of IODA in 1965 the (non-technical) Rules stated "identical building plans should be obligatory for all members - *with certain exceptions for USA*".

The actual hull dimensions changed little. When Nigel Ringrose came to transfer the metric dimensions of the Danish plans (Britain did not start metrication until the mid-60s) he recalls: "I remember my puzzlement when finding that the measurements would always divide neatly by 2.54 i.e. equal to USA/British inches". The biggest change was that the hull was made lighter by, for example, replacing the 3/4"/18*mm transoms with 12mm ply. According to Michael Ranson's excellent history of the U.K. Class 1960-1980, *The Greatest Little Boat in the World*, now sadly out of print, the original weight of the 'British Optimist' was 27.2kg, increased in 1969 to 33kg and by 1972 to 35kg.

The foils were reduced in thickness. The daggerboard, planed down from 1"/25.4mm cypress in the prototype and using 3/4"/18*mm plywood in the 1955 pram plans, was reduced in thickness to 12mm plywood. The maximum width of the slot, 1"/25.4mm on the pram, was reduced to 16mm. The rudder thickness was also reduced from 3/4"/18*mm to 12mm. The external dimensions of the daggerboard were left unchanged (though the diagonal edges were discontinued in both the pram and the Optimist) but the vertical length of the rudder was increased from 660mm (26") to 750mm (29.5") and the width reduced from 292mm to 260mm. The actual rudder shape was not prescribed in either boat and remained undefined until the next century.
* 3/4" is in fact 19mm but the closest standard plywood thickness is quoted.

Perhaps most important were the changes in the sail. Whereas the pram rules stated clearly that "all sails must be flat cut and composed of three panels with seams parallel to the leach [sic]" the Danes introduced battens and lateral panels while abolishing the 'flat cut' rule. The Danish plans also permitted the sail to extend beyond a straight line drawn from the peak to the clew and this, at least by 1971, increased the half-width by around 20%, and sails were now tied to the boom.

The basic dimensions of the sail were also increased as follows

	Pram	Optimist
Luff	1676	1730
Head	1219	1240
Foot	1981	2130
Peak to Clew	2667	2800
Diagonal	2464	2580

Dacron was permitted and the Optimist exhibited at the 1961 London Boat Show is recorded as having a "varnished terylene" sail. Cotton remains a theoretical option even today.

The length of the mast was increased from 2290mm to 2350mm to match the new luff but the length of the boom and sprit were left unchanged. More surprisingly the spar diameters were left unchanged in the 1961 plans, though circular sections were permitted. Only around 1970 was the mast diameter increased from 41.3mm to 45mm and the sprit from 19mm to 24mm. The boom however remained at 25mm.

It appears that it was the British who first added buoyancy, absent from the Clearwater pram, the Danish Optimist in the museum and the first imported hull. At the 1961 British Championships one of the few rules was "At least two separate buoyancy units, together supporting at least 100lb [44.6kg] must be securely fitted to the boat." Further work on this was done by physicist Pierre Lostis from

Aberwrac'h in Brittany and three buoyancy units supporting 60kg became the standard. Initially polystyrene foam was permitted as an alternative to buoyancy bags but this was later permitted only if encased within built-in boxes (as shown in the Esgrus photo).

Important improvements later in the 1960s were:

- Toe straps: permitted from 1968. Tiller extensions reportedly introduced around the same time.
- Ratchet blocks for the mainsheet, first allowed in 1969.
- A transparent sail window, allowed in the 1971 rules but not seen on photos from the mid-1970s.
- While early pictures from Clearwater show mast-head ribbons, such devices do not appear in the Class Rules; other wind-indicators were not permitted until 1980.

Great Britain

In 1960 the British sailor Nigel Ringrose, while sailing his Shearwater catamaran, came across the

Nigel

Optimists in Vordingborg, imported one for a cousin and started building them as a hobby. He re-wrote the Danish rules in English and established a fleet at his grandmother's house at Bursledon on the Hamble river.

Despite showing at the London Boat Show at Earl's Court in late 1961 there was little interest from established yacht clubs, with the honourable exception of the Royal Southern. The first commercially produced boats were made by Moores of Wroxham who in fact were to continue to build in wood and later GRP until 1998. They also supplied kits and more seem to have been built by private builders in the U.K. than elsewhere. Perhaps due to competition from the Cadet and Mirror dinghies, 'only' around 120 were sold in the first two years As late as 1967 it was recorded that: "Virtually all Optimists . . . were in Hampshire or nearby" and by the end of the decade less than 700

OP-1

sail numbers had been issued.

The first 'Worlds'

Two years later Nigel invited the Danes, Swedes and Germans (though only the first two attended) to the first 'International Optimist Regatta' which is now regarded as the first World Championship. The Beacon Cup, still awarded to the champion, had in fact been used for the British Nationals in 1961 but in future was used for the international event.

Scandinavian sailors dominated and did much to convince doubters of the seaworthiness of the boat. The winner was the tiny Anders Quiding (see photo) followed by Peter Due, a later Tornado Olympic silver medallist from Århus.

The following year the Swedes returned the invitation by inviting the British to the second 'International Regatta' which was held in Göteborg, this time including Norway to give a five-nation event. Not surprisingly the third regatta was held in Viggo's home town of Århus. The USA was enticed across the pond - and won the team prize - to give a seven-nation championship.

Some of the participants in 1962.
The British team is in the front row

The Swedish team 1962. Second from the left
is the winner Anders Quiding next to his father

The Danish team 1962. Second from the right
is silver medallist Peter Due

Growth in the '60s

Geographical spread thereafter was incredible. The years in which Optimists were introduced by the other countries (as reported in a questionnaire circulated in 1980 unless there is clear evidence to the contrary) were as follows:

1959   Norway
1960   Great Britain*, Sweden*
1962   Germany*, Rhodesia*
1963   Finland
1965   Austria, Belgium*, Bulgaria, Greece*, Italy
1966   France*, Japan, Poland
1967   Venezuela
1968   Ireland§, Monaco, South Africa, Czechoslovakia
1969   Argentina*, Bermuda, Spain*, Turkey*, Switzerland
1970   Morocco*

* the countries which, with USA and Denmark, supported the 1970 application for International status (see below)

§ But East Antrim B.C. and Carrickfergus Y.C. in Northern Ireland had introduced Optimists as early as 1964-5.

Note that in many cases there were individual Optimists built before the dates shown.

Germany

The introduction to Germany resulted from a demonstration by Danish sailors at the Warnemünder week regatta in 1961. Eight Optimists were built and in the following year a joint regatta was held. Political separation could not keep a good idea down and building started almost immediately at Rerik on the Salzhaff in the DDR ('East' Germany). Growth thereafter was phenomenal with, for example, clubs in Schleswig building sixty Optimists in 1963 and holding an 80-boat regatta with the Danes, attended by Viggo, the following year. Contact with the DDR was difficult but future winner of four Olympic medals Jochen Schümann records that *"In 1965 I took a school vacation course on 'boatbuilding & sailing' in Berlin-Köpenick, where I helped building Optimists. I started sailing those Optimists in 1966."*

Finland

The introduction to Finland may have been earlier. Despite rapid growth the Finnish Yachting Association was reluctant to accept the new dinghy, reputedly on the grounds that many of them carried advertising. This debate about advertising in the sport of sailing was to continue internationally for many years and only recently may have been finally resolved.

and beyond

Austria actually participated in the 'International Regatta' in 1965 *before* they had any Optimists at home. Following the trip described below, Kurt and Erika Olga Jirasko from the Neusiedlersee Y.C. invested their entire savings in importing 20 Danish boats, price at that time ÖS 4,500 each [USD 173, about $460 in 2012 terms - *Ed*] and on 24th April 1966 the first Optimist Club was founded.

After what might be regarded as the 'contagious' spread in Scandinavia and onwards to Germany and Austria, it is interesting that two of the next introductions were by National Sailing Associations in communist Bulgaria and in Greece where the Hellenic Yachting Federation had the vision to import

120 wooden 'Hannibal' Optimists in 1965. In Italy the first fleets were in Liguria and Lake Garda but, like the Balkans but unlike Scandinavia, for the first ten years boats were mostly owned by clubs and used primarily for training.

The idea of junior sailboat racing was regarded with some suspicion. The 1980 Italian report noted that "according to Italian law no young people under 14 years of age can start in any competition" which may be why even today some Italian regattas are still called 'meetings'. Austria too reported that "the Austrian Sailing Association . . . has a strong policy against children sailing races." This was a theme which would recur intermittently for many years.

France, starting in 1966 under the aegis of Jo Chartois, director of the *Ecole Nationale de Voile* in Carantec, took enthusiastically to the *caisse à savon,* sailed in the Worlds of 1967 and hosted the 1968 Worlds in Carantec. By the time of its 1980 report POP ("an independent institution recognised by the National Authority F.F.V.") boasted "about 20,000 Optimists", second only to Sweden. At that time boats were privately owned though "some wealthy clubs put very good boats at the disposal of young sailors".

Poland too developed rapidly with about 1,500 boats by 1980. IODA knew nothing of the USSR but the Poles reported that they participated in "great regattas organized by the socialistic countries." Intriguingly the 1980 report from Hungary mentioned an Optimist training book in Russian published in Estonia in 1966.

Japan

Outside Europe Japan was the first Asian country to acquire Optimists, influenced by another Dane, Kaj Wolhardt (grandfather of 1967/8 world champion Peter Warrer) and led by the charismatic Ben Majima but numbers by 1980 were only 300.

Africa

In Africa a fleet had existed since 1962 in Rhodesia, introduced by Andrew Huddleston, and a Class association since 1964. In 1967 Nigel was posted to Pietermaritzburg in Natal and soon had the first fleet of South African Optimists sailing on the nearby Midmar Dam. By 1974 they sailed in the Optimist Worlds and proudly reported that they were the best-placed English speakers "beating out the super confident and organised Americans and Brits". Sadly however for fifteen years from 1976 their teams usually encountered problems with entry to World and European Championships.

South America

Little is known about the early fleet in Venezuela but the breakthrough in Argentina was also helped by Nigel Ringrose, working with Hugo Tedim and Hugh Warneford-Thomson of the Y.C. Argentino, who had imported two British Optimists in 1968. Plans for the first boats built in Argentina were bought by naval architect Patricio Billoch and built by Jorge Cavado. Patricio's son Martín owned A-1 and was to win the Worlds the first time Argentina participated in 1974 on the Silvaplana, Switzerland. As well as Martín, who went on to become a very influential boat designer, the initial group included (A-3) future Olympic medallist and GRP Optimist builder Santiago Lange. The yacht clubs of San Fernando, Olivos and San Isidro followed quickly and the first national

A-1: Martín Billoch

championship with 19 boats was held in 1971, followed in 1973 by the first South American Championship.

Spain

Back in Europe Optimists were shown at the Barcelona Boat Show of 1968. Spain's sailors participated in the 1968 Worlds (now definitely so called) in Carantec but had warned the organisers that they were only present "to learn and to make contact with the little world of the Optimist which extends to five continents". Nevertheless they finished ahead of Venezuela, Great Britain, Belgium and Germany. Within a year the original fleets in R.C.N. Barcelona and Arenys del Mar had expanded to Bilbao, Malaga and Madrid, 150 boats in all, and the following year even as far as Ibiza where in July a blessing of the boats was attended by one Juan Antonio Samaranch *delegado nacional de Educacion Fisica y Deportes*. Arenys hosted the Worlds of 1970. Just two years later Spain broke the Scandinavian/USA duopoly of victors when Tomás Estela from Palma de Mallorca won the Worlds of 1972 and Spain the team prize . . . in Sweden.

Tomás was one of the first ex-Optimists to shine at the IYRU Youth World Championships, founded in 1971, where he took gold in the 420s in 1974 and silver in 1975.

The International Optimist Dinghy Association

The International Optimist Dinghy Association (IODA) was founded at the fourth Regatta in 1965 in Turku in Finland. The first members were Austria, Denmark, Finland, Great Britain, Norway, Sweden and USA, followed shortly by Germany and Rhodesia (Zimbabwe).

The new association brought together the work of Viggo Jacobsen, who was elected president, and that of Nigel Ringrose as vice-president. These two were to remain in those positions for over

Viggo & Edith

15 years with Viggo's English-born wife Edith as honorary secretary.

Viggo was an ideal president. He had been trained in woodworking and had even owned a small boatbuilding company before the war. He had then joined the family paper-merchant business. As a Dragon sailor - like many of the most influential yachtsmen of his generation - he knew one-design sailing. Among other activities he organised the Århus Boat Show, the profits of which were used to fund junior sailing (after a loss in the first year). Bent Lyman's comment that he was a 'foreign minister' acquired a wider meaning as he worked tirelessly with the various national groups as the Optimist spread.

Nigel was a great roving ambassador. "*He worked for the United Nations and set up Opti programs wherever he went around the world. He came here and said "why don't you guys have any Optis here?"* was the typical report of Connecticut's Sinclair.

Ivar Ahlgren from Långedrags SS in Göteborg, president of the newly formed Swedish Optimist Association, became the auditor, a position he was to hold for over thirty years. Understandably apart from Nigel most of

Viggo & Nigel

the leading lights of the new IODA were for many years Scandinavian, among them Lars Wallin, Eric Carsten Hansen and Jens Andersen as chairmen of the IODA Technical Committee. None of these were current Optimist parents which gave a consistency and strength seen in few other Classes.

The International Regatta in the 60s

Title:

It is not entirely clear when the 'International Optimist Regatta' started to be called a World Championship. Certainly the 1967 event in Austria was not so called - but the Austrian sailing authorities were not that happy at there being any such event - and equally the 1968 it was so called, at least by the Spanish press when recording the first national participation at the event. According to Nigel, neither he nor Viggo liked the idea of a 15-year old world champion but the word 'World' was critical in attracting sponsorship for the organisers of a rapidly growing event.

Teams:

Nigel's invitation to the first 'International Optimist Regatta' had been for four or five sailors and it seems that official teams were established from the start as four plus a reserve. The International Team Trophy, later the IODA Challenge Cup, was based on the aggregate scores of the best four sailors in a series of five races "sailed under IYRU teamracing rules" and for many years was regarded as the primary world championship in line with Nigel's original concept to "encourage team spirit rather than individualism". The Beacon Cup for the individual championship, also five races, had in fact been donated the previous year for the British Nationals. A further trophy, the Miami Herald dating from 1966, was initially awarded for a single race between Denmark, USA, the host country and the two best teams from the Challenge Cup.

There was considerable demand for extra places and an additional secondary *open* competition was soon introduced for the Prins Bertils Cup (donated by a Swedish company which owned a vessel of that name). It continued in various forms, usually as a separate single race, until around 1988, after which extra sailors were no longer allowed. By then the IODA European championship was providing an alternative for those who did not make the first national team. The Prins Bertils Cup was later awarded for the silver fleet until splitting the fleet was discontinued in 1992.

Entry:

The age limit for participants was debated for many years. The original 1948 Pram Rules were under-15 at the time of racing. By 1969 it was "Competitors must not have reached the age of 17 before 15th August" but in the following year this was replaced by the year of birth and in 1972 reduced to under-16. Discussions of the best age limit continued for several years but it was finally confirmed in 1981 as under-16 in the calendar year. Weight and height were factors in the debate but so was social maturity. Clark Mills had given a blunter contribution from the start: "*All of a sudden in two to three years a kid can turn into a monster. Not all of them but a lot of them - too many greaseburgers I guess.*"

From an early stage the entry fee included accommodation and meals. This gave the young people the experience of Hogwarts-style communal living and the chance to socialise with sailors from other countries. It also enabled teams to budget more accurately. The idea was adopted for the IYRU Youth World Championship when that event was created in 1971. Initially only two adults were allowed in this accommodation, later expanded to three; any other parents and coaches had to stay elsewhere.

There have been occasional problems. Some teams wanted to bring their own camper-wagons and food, and an occasional wealthy team booked into the nearest luxury hotel, but IODA stuck rigidly to an inclusive entry fee. Some National Authorities perversely complained that the entry fee was higher than for other Classes where sailors found their own lodgings. However the principle survived and was later extended to most continental championships, at least as these became limited to official teams.

Sail Letters & Numbers:

Many early continental European Optimists carried letters and numbers which seem to have been issued at club level (see the photo of Peter Warrer). However the British used the sail letters 'OP' with consecutive numbers which they also supplied to an number of other Anglophone countries, even for boats built in those countries. The first picture where the Optimist logo can be seen outside the USA seems to have been that of the 1971 Worlds in Malente (see next chapter) and this use may have originated when IODA was in negotiations with Clearwater about copyright during the application for IYRU status.

The use of national letters appears to have started around 1968, certainly before the Optimist became an IYRU International Class. At that time the IYRU used national letters which had originated around 1925 and reflected their British origin. 'K' was used for Great Britain and most British Commonwealth countries had sail letters starting with a 'K', for example 'KC' for Canada. 'H' was used for what the British called Holland but some of the other letters are difficult to understand: why 'Z' for Switzerland? Not until 1993 did the IYRU change to the three-letter Olympic abbreviations though it still lists these as if issued by it.

Some regattas

A rare description of one of the early 'Worlds' comes from Austria, the experience of Kurt and Erika-Olga Jirasko from the Neusiedlersee Y.C. They had heard of the Optimists in Denmark and in 1965 the couple travelled with two children to Finland where the Optimist Championship was being held. Boats were supplied and the two sailors 'joined the party'. "It blew Force eight" remembers Erika-Olga "and I was terribly afraid for the welfare of my protegés". Unnecessarily as it turned out: the kids just did their own thing in the exceptionally stable *Kiste* (crates). Frau Jirasko was so impressed with the boat and the enthusiasm of the little sailors that she almost without thinking offered to host the 1967 event in Austria.

Before it could be held, there was a legal problem because at that time in Austria young people were not allowed to sail single-handed. At the event itself a heatwave hit the 61 participants from eleven countries. One little Finn wrote to his mother: "It is as hot as India but they don't have any elephants!"

Among the Austrian participants - in 30th place - was nine-year old Wolfgang Mayrhofer who, just thirteen years later, was to win Olympic silver in the Finn Class.

Getting to the Neusiedlersee was not without its problems. In the days of limited charter availability, high air-fares and customs barriers, travel was problem. The British reported a journey by train with "six Optimists as our luggage in the guard's van . . . and a vast amount of paperwork in advance as well as a lot of man-handling on the way". Nevertheless the number of countries represented reached double figures for the first time and the first participation of Rhodesia and Venezuela meant four continents.

The 1969 'International Regatta' (the British still did not accept the title 'Worlds') almost did not take place due to difficulties with funding. Finally sponsorship of £3,500 was found, arranged almost inevitably by the Ringrose family.

Results:

As shown in the table below the early years were dominated by sailors from the big fleets of Sweden and Denmark, with the occasional success of the Floridans.

Year	Venue	Countries		Winner		Team
1962	Hamble	GBR	3	Anders Quiding	SWE	SWE
1963	Göteborg	SWE	5	B.Baysen	SWE	SWE
1964	Århus	DEN	7	Poul Andersen	DEN	USA
1965	Turku	FIN	9	Ray Larsson	SWE	FIN
1966	Miami	USA	6	Doug Bull	USA	SWE
1967	Neusiedlersee	AUT	11	Peter Warrer	DEN	DEN
1968	Carantec	FRA	13	Peter Warrer	DEN	DEN
1969	Stokes Bay	GBR	12	Doug Bull	USA	USA

Peter Warrer (DEN)
World Champion
1967 & 1968

Notes on Chapters 2 & 3

Sources:

The Greatest Little Boat in the World - the Story of the Optimist in the United Kingdom 1960-1990 by Michael Ranson

Correspondence with Nigel Ringrose

Memories about Axel Damgaard Olsen, the OK co-designer by Gerald Elfendahl 1998 at http://www.okdia.org/association/history_a_d_olsen.php

Archive of the Danmarks Museum for Lystsejlads including the articles
Optimist-jolle fra ca.1960 by Bent Lyman
Viggo Jacobsen, Optimist-jollens "udenrigsminister" by Bent Lyman
PG - en pioner i dansk sejlsport by Henrik Hansen

Material from the Optimist Museum in Esgrus, Germany

100 Year Anniversary Publication of Yacht Club of Turku, Finland

El Mundo Deportivo, La Vanguardia (10 July 1976) and *Placar* magazines online

Les 50 ans du Centre Nautique de Douarnenez-Tréboul online

The Ditty Bag August 2006. Article *"Catching up with David Sinclair"*.

St. Petersburg Y.C. Juniors Web (www.spyc.org/files/6%20juniors-web.pdf)

Porträt 50 Jahre OPTIMIST by Judith Duller-Mayrhofer in *Yacht Review*

Deutschlands Optimisten – die Geschichte einer tollen Kiste by Nadja Arp

Archive of the Optimist Club Denmark

List of British measurement certificates supplied by the RYA

Chapter 3: The 1970s

IYRU Recognition

In 1970 IODA applied to the International Yacht Racing Union (IYRU) for the status of 'International Class'. In fact the boat had been called the International Optimist at least as early as 1961.

Relatively few Classes already had that status which, even as late as 1986, required at least 1,500 boats worldwide with fleets of at least 50 actively racing in 11 countries, and 6 nations at the Worlds. The Optimist qualified easily on this numeric basis with 13 countries (see above) supporting the application and 12 at the 1970 Worlds.

However at that time and for many years afterwards IYRU Regulations specified that: "The new class shall not be adopted if it is considered that it will adversely affect an existing International Class" and, as reported by Nigel, opposition came from supporters of the British-designed International Cadet, adopted in 1958, despite that being a two-person boat. Support for IODA's application nevertheless came from IYRU Secretary-General Nigel Hacking and Chief Measurer Tony Watts.

A further problem lay in ownership of the copyright. At that time the main requirement for International Class status was transfer of the design copyright (though it was and is somewhat questionable as to whether copyright law applies in many countries to the design of non-artistic products) and it was very debatable as to who owned any Optimist copyright. Clark Mills had designed a boat but had transferred any intellectual property to the Optimist Club of Clearwater. The Danes had altered the plans and negotiated with Clearwater the use of the name 'Danish optimistdinghy'. The British had reportedly registered the copyright on the 'British building plans (1961, revised 1966)'. Most existing International Classes had a single named designer such as Jack Holt (Cadet, GP14, Enterprise and Mirror) or Christian Maury (420) who received a royalty on boats built. But the Optimist had been changed and evolved in Denmark and England. Finally it was agreed that the building fee paid per boat would be split 37.5% each to the IYRU and IODA and 25% to the National Optimist Association, with no payment to any possible copyright holder.

The Class Rules too were not of the standard required by the IYRU. The Danish plans which Nigel had translated were revised by Edmund Spalding, at the time head of the IODA Technical Committee. Spalding wrote: *"Eventually at the [1972] IODA AGM in Sweden a draft of the Rules was agreed. When I got home I prepared a final draft and sent a copy to all member countries. I enclosed a letter to say that if no objections were received within TEN days acceptance would be assumed. None was received so this second draft was submitted to the IYRU."* Finally after further inquisition by the Union the Optimist became officially international from March 1st 1973.

Technical Developments

British records show that as early as 1967 a GRP boat was built by the firm Polyastic. At the 1969 London Boat Show permission was given to show "a GRP boat imported from France provided that it was styled an 'Experimental Optimist '." Later that same year a Danish Henriksen was shown at the Worlds "for evaluation and measurement" and manufacture of the GRP hull was officially approved by IODA from January 1st 1970, provided that "it was not inferior to a wooden boat in regard to safety, strength and buoyancy". Interestingly the 1971 Class Rules attempted to specify the weights and standard of the laminates but these could not be easily measured and disappeared

Low quality GRP and wooden Optimists (1976)

Note the oars. A rowing seat could be fitted in the trunk.

from the Rules shortly thereafter.

The following years saw a free-for-all in the development of GRP Optimists, not least because of the wide range of options permitted; for example: "the bottom of the boat may be single, single with stringers, double, or a combination of these" (1976 Rules). These early GRP boats tended to be heavy and slow but there was a rapidly expanding market. Especially in sailing schools, maintenance costs were seen as lower than for wood. Customs barriers were still high, even in Europe, and, if government or National Sailing Association money was involved, a local manufacturer who could supply in volume was preferred. It was much easier to order a batch of GRP boats than the careful building of large numbers of wooden Optimists.

Many of these boats did not conform to such GRP Class Rules as existed. In February 1978 Viggo issued a circular:

"During the winter of 1975-76 members of the IODA Technical Committee visited three European Boat Shows and found that all was not well with the little boat. It was decided therefore [in] 1976-77 to visit five of the larger Boat Shows and we came across the real gravity of the problem with 'empty cavities'. As can be understood we were not always received very friendly when we told the exhibitor . . . that these were absolutely not Optimist dinghies."

This circular highlighted two problems.

Firstly while the Technical Committee could apparently identify what were *not* Optimists when it saw them, such GRP plans as existed left builders great freedom as to what they built. As late as 1982 the minutes of the IODA AGM resolved that a "One-Design GRP hull plan [is] to be developed for submission to the 1983 AGM" and the 1983 IODA Yearbook stated that: "The hull may be built of wood, glass reinforced plastic, ABS plastic and self-skinning polyurethane foam". Neither statement suggests clear guidance to builders as to what was and what was not permitted.

The efforts to define what was and what was not an Optimist were assisted by Tony Watts, the Chief Measurer of the IYRU. It was probably he who proposed the idea of a 'Certificate of General Approval' for builders to be issued by the IYRU but there is little evidence that many of these were issued.

Second was a situation which has never been totally resolved. National associations and parents often sought boats, at as low a cost as possible, simply to teach sailing. They did not appreciate that very soon the pupils from these 'learn to sail' programmes would want to go racing . . . and racing demanded boats which were more or less equal in specification and speed.

Typical was the experience of Yugoslavia:

"With the help of our own builders in 1975-6 we were able to supply the dinghies for every yacht club in Yugoslavia. We didn't give much attention to the quality but after the World Championship in Turkey 1976 we were forced to think about better boats."

Those "better boats" might have come from a number of builders such as Copino in Spain, Henriksen in Denmark and various French builders, but they were probably thinking of Falsleds. In 1974 that

Danish company launched a twin-walled Optimist with a GRP outer shell and an orange ABS-moulded inner shell, incorporating foam-filled buoyancy tanks. After an reported initial setback when an error of 30mm was reportedly found in the bow transom, the new boat was established to be as fast as most if not all wooden boats.

The impact of these competitive GRP boats could upset national fleets. Turkey had already over a thousand boats, many sponsored for club use by the Turkish Y.A., and was faced with the arrival of fast imported Falsleds "bought by rich parents". Italy reported: "Optimist building in Italy is limited today to a few small shipyards while as to [competitive] activity Danish, Spanish and French dinghies are normally used." In the same year the Hellenic Yachting Federation reported that it mostly imported French or, later, Danish boats.

The building of wooden boats continued, not least because they were still winning the Worlds in the hands of talented Swedes such as Johan Petterson, winner in 1979 and 80. As late as 1979 over 40% of Optimists registered in the British market were still wooden.

It is easy to be romantic about wooden boats built on the kitchen table. The reality is that in most countries the majority were built by commercial builders but expert parents or those 'in the know' always had an advantage. One future Olympic medallist wrote of another, a club-mate who won the Optimist Worlds: *"Dad built me a wooden Optimist. But [xxxxxx] always had the finest, fastest wooden Optimists."* Note the plural: they often didn't last that long in top condition, not least because there were known problems with the quality of marine plywood which did not even necessarily comply with quality marks.

Falsled dominance of the market for competitive GRP Optimists was to be relatively short-lived due to the arrival of the rival Winner Optimist but that was mostly in the next decade.

Spars

One unquestionable improvement was the introduction in 1973 of aluminium alloy spars. At the 1971 Worlds it was reported that: "the wind became so strong that our masts (of wood of course) snapped faster than matches. We had to buy new ones and bind them with fibreglass tape. They must have been the heaviest masts ever but, with reinforcement, there were no more breakages". The earliest known manufacturer in the U.K. was Needlespars. By 1978 Båths in Sweden were offering the Tecnospar, a "racing rig incorporating a high tensile aircraft alloy".

Sails

In the mid-'70s coloured sails disappeared from competition boats. This seems to have been partly to avoid being easily identified as OCS, but also due to lighter-weight sailcloth being available only in white.

Towards a wider world

While the number of national fleets in Europe continued to increase, the main expansion especially in the later '70s was outside Europe.

The growth, as reported in 1980, was as follows:

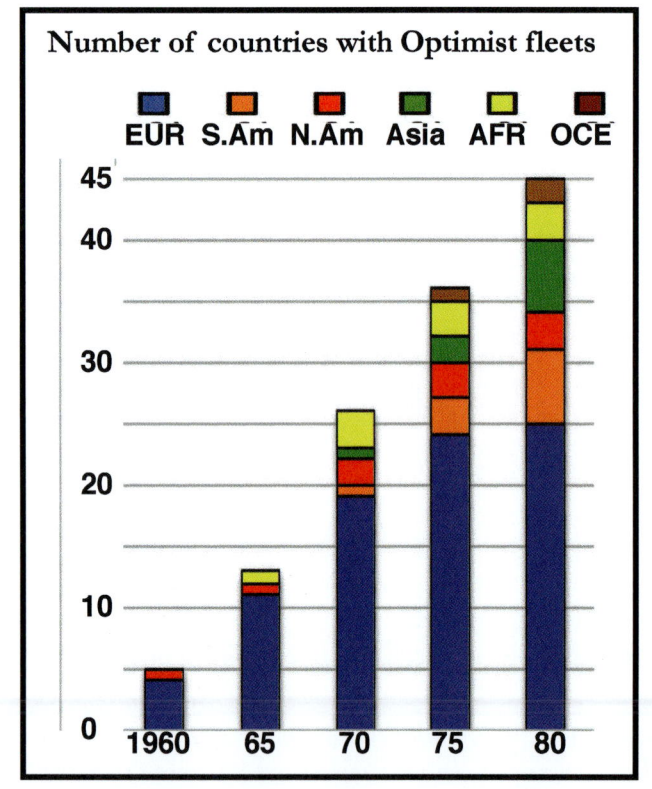

Number of countries with Optimist fleets

EUR S.Am N.Am Asia AFR OCE

1972	Brasil, Hungary
1976	Uruguay
1973	Canada, Netherlands, Portugal
1977	Thailand, Korea
1974	Iceland, Yugoslavia
1978	Australia, Peru, Singapore
1975	Colombia, India, New Zealand
1980	Chile

Dates unknown:

Indonesia: listed as a member in 1980.

Romania: by 1979 were participating successfully in a Balkan regatta.

Thus by 1980 IODA listed 45 members.

The Optimist was introduced to Brasil in 1972 by triple Finn Olympian Jörg Bruder (who was tragically killed in a plane crash the following year) and Sibylle Sulzbeck from São Paolo. Within Brasil the Class spread rapidly through the vast country with over a dozen centres by 1980 from Fortaleza to Porto Alegre. By 1980, 1,150 registered Optimists were reported, as many as Argentina which had started earlier

Uruguay followed shortly afterwards, hosting the South Americans for the first time in 1978. In Peru the sea scouts in Callao built their first Optimists in the same year but the country did not participate in the South Americans for another eight years. In Europe Hungary started building and soon began fleets on Balaton and Lake Velence. The Optimist Club Nederland was established by Anders Pels whose son Jeroen (Jerome) sailed in three IODA Worlds and has gone on to become CEO of the ISAF. Portugal imported boats from Spain with the first fleets in Cascais, which was to host the Worlds in 1980, Oporto and Aveiro. While India was the second Asian country to start Optimists, at the College of Military Engineering in Pune, more immediate impact came from the foundation in January 1977 of the Junior Sailing Squadron of Thailand with the help of Al Chandler, an American

lawyer resident in Bangkok. Al worked closely with the Thai navy but it was noted that "funding for its program has been raised from the private sector" and, as in the early days in Florida, sponsors of boats were allowed extensive advertising. By 1979 150 wooden Optimists had been built locally which enabled the world championship to be hosted in Pattaya. Al, like Nigel, travelled extensively and was soon spreading the gospel throughout Asia, crucially to Singapore.

Growth of the World Championship

The growth in numbers of fleets was matched by the growth of the Worlds. While in 1968 the popular venue of Brittany had attracted 13 teams, ten years later it saw 25. Understandably numbers fell in 1979 with the bold step of taking the Worlds to Thailand but this first visit to Asia led to Australia, India, Japan, Pakistan and Singapore participating for the first time. However of these only Japan was to compete in the following years when the event returned to Europe. Air fares were still very high: the USD600 'special fare' arranged from Copenhagen to Bangkok in 1979 equals nearly USD2,200 in 2012 terms, well over twice the 2012 price.

Not all countries could attend every year. Morocco, for example, attended in Spain in 1970 and Bermuda in 1974 in St. Moritz.

The championships were not without their problems. In Malente near Kiel in 1971 accommodation was in army tents and the food and the weather were, according to the British team-leader, grim. An ongoing problem which was to recur was that the few girls often had to share with members of other teams. The 1973 Worlds scheduled for Rhodesia/Zimbabwe had to be cancelled due to security and perhaps boycott worries. In St. Moritz in 1974 a day was lost to requests for redress and protests. In La Baule in 1978 the French insisted on almost unlimited 'open' entry resulting in 226 sailors participating in the single Prins Bertils race.

A major problem was identified in the 1980 report from Dieter Roos, president of the German DODV: *"A very important cost element is the dinghy transport expenses. We think these expenses are avoidable if the dinghies would be provided for all competitors and if possible only dinghies of the same manufacturer."*

Charter boats were in fact generally available but the quality was unknown and any team in a position to do so transported their own boats. For Thailand in 1979 eight of the 13 non-Asian countries did so. Those which did not, such as Spain, complained that some of the locally built Thai boats were reportedly up to 6kg over-weight. The following year in Cascais the Irish team reported that the charter boats literally fell apart. In Howth in 1981 the Falsled charter boats, while of excellent quality, were a model which had recently become outdated by developments described elsewhere. The problem would only be solved by developments in GRP boats and charter arrangements in the next decade.

Scandinavia, and in particular Sweden, continued to dominate the championship

World Championships 1970-9						
	Venue		Countries	Champion		Team
1970	Arenys	ESP	14	James Larimore	USA	SWE
1971	Malente	GER	12	Heiki Vahtera	FIN	SWE
1972	Karlskrona	SWE	15	Tomás Estela	ESP	ESP
1973	Cancelled due to problems in Rhodesia					
1974	St. Moritz	SUI	20	Martín Billoch	ARG	SWE
1975	Århus	DEN	23	Hans Fester	SWE	DEN
1976	Yarimka	TUR	19	Hans Wallén	SWE	SWE
1977	Koper	YUG	22	Patrik Mark	SWE	DEN
1978	La Baule	FRA	25	Rikard Hammarvid	SWE	SWE
1979	Pattaya	THA	17	Johan Petterson	SWE	SWE

Malente, Germany - 1971

St. Moritz, Switzerland - 1974

Yarimka, Turkey - 1976

The first continental championships

The earliest was the South Americans, created in 1973 shortly after Brasil had started with Optimists. Three of the first four sailors at that initial event were to go on to represent Argentina at the Olympics: Gonzalo Campero in the Finn, Martín Billoch in the 470 and, most successfully, Santiago Lange who has sailed in five Games and won two Tornado bronze medals. The second edition was won by a USA sailor, Richard St. John, but this would not happen often in the future. Uruguay joined in 1976 and hosted the event in 1978.

South American Championships 1973-9				
	Venue		*Champion*	*Team*
1973	San Isidro	ARG	Gonzalo Campero	ARG
1974	Rio de Janeiro	BRA	John King	BRA
1975	San Isidro	ARG	Hugo Castro	ARG
1976	João Pessoa	BRA	Eduardo Melchert	BRA
1977	San Isidro	ARG	Guillermo Baquerizas	ARG
1978	Puerto Buceo	URU	Gustavo Warburg	ARG
1979	Capao de Canoa	BRA	Mariano Castro	ARG

In North America the first truly international Optimist North Americans seems to have been organised in 1976 at St. Petersburg Y.C. by Richard Merriman. Participants included sailors representing Bermuda, Venezuela, and Canada which by this stage had Optimists in both Toronto and Quebec. The USA sailors were from Florida (St. Petersburg, Miami and Fort Lauderdale) and racing was provided for what was described as the 'Optimist pram' as well as the 'Optimist dinghy'. While all the USA sailors in 1976 were from Florida, by 1979 when the championship was hosted by the Royal Canadian Y.C. in Toronto it was recorded that "about a dozen USA skippers from Connecticut and Florida participated". No results sheets have been found but it is believed that winners included Rick Merriman (?1976) and Mike Funsch (?1979) both from St. Petersburg Y.C

The Evening Independent - Jan 17, 1976

KATE STOWELL
Scene Editor

If you happened down by the St. Petersburg Junior Yacht Club last weekend, you would have been embroiled in a tangle of activity. Beginning Friday morning, young people between the ages of 9 and 15 were hard at work preparing sailboats. And on Saturday, they got their chance to sail those boats in a first-ever championship.

It was the North American International Optimist Dinghy Championship, and it brought together young people from St. Petersburg, Miami, Fort Lauderdale, Bermuda, Canada and Venezuela. The championship was a first, explains Richard Merriman, junior activities chairman for the St. Petersburg Yacht Club, because it was the first international event in the dinghy class.

"The International Optimist Dinghy Association is an international association," explained Merriman. "We sent invitations to all groups. The world championship is held in Europe. Only kids 9 to 14 may participate. And strangely enough, there are more of these boats (Optimist dinghys) in the world than any other sailboats."

The two types of boats sailed on Saturday included the Optimist dinghy and the Optimist pram, which originally was designed in Clearwater. Many of the participants brought their own boats, but others borrowed from non-participating clubs such as Bradenton.

So when the wind kicked up brisk and breezy Saturday, championship participants were ready to tackle the sails in hopes of taking home a winning trophy. But most of them were more interested in racing simply for the experience, rather than for winning. "It teaches them to make their own decisions and it builds self-confidence," explained Merriman.

The contestants themselves spoke of the Olympic course, 5-mile race a little differently.

"This is my first international event," explained Christopher Bardgett, 13, of Bermuda. "I've been sailing for three years. Last year I was supposed to go to the world championship but it was canceled. It really doesn't matter if I get a trophy, because I participated. My dad has sailed for 30-odd years so I want to see if I can follow in his footsteps."

Viggo's Legacy

Thus by 1980 Optimists were firmly established throughout Europe, even if little was known about the 'East Block'. Outside Europe there were several significant fleets and obvious potential for further growth in Asia and South America.

On the technical side IODA was moving towards the transition, difficult for all Classes, from wood to GRP construction.

Viggo may have been in Paul Elvstrøm's mind when the latter famously wrote: "It is easier to design a new boat than build a sustainable Class organisation". As a businessman Viggo had looked at realities and shaped policies around them. He had reservations about GRP boats, about the need for the title 'world champion' and even, according to Nigel, about the usefulness of the IYRU, but he had been willing to negotiate all of them.

Clark had built a boat. Viggo had built a Class.

Chapter 4: The 1980s

In 1981 Viggo Jacobsen retired. *"Nothing can last forever. As a leader you ought to lay down the reins while still in control of the horses"* he said in an interview. Continuity was ensured not only by the succession of Nigel Ringrose as president but by the appointment of Hanne Rix as the Class's first professional secretary. It was she who, operating her own office services company in the same building as Viggo's office, had in fact already been doing much of the routine IODA work. So international had IODA become she even installed a fax machine, the height of technology at the time.

Hanne with Jes Retbøll, treasurer and later vice-president

Eric Hansen, who had already been a member of the Technical Committee for many years took over the chair of that committee from Lars Wallin and was shortly to become one of the first IYRU International Measurers. The vice-presidents were Jorma Heiskanen of Finland and Al Chandler from Thailand.

Nigel, Al, Eric & Jes

The following year IODA was further strengthened by the creation of a Regatta Committee (which had been proposed as long before as 1978) to assist the organisation of the World Championship. With Al as chair, the members included Helen Mary Wilkes and Michel Barbier, significant names for the future of IODA.

Nigel was re-elected in 1983 but he was now working for the United Nations in Bangladesh and, despite that fax machine, communications were very difficult and in 1985 he retired. Al Chandler moved to the presidency and Helen Mary Wilkes was elected as vice-president and chair of the Regatta Committee. Jorma Heiskanen (FIN) decided to follow his children into the Europe Class, of which he was to become the long-term president, and two new vice-presidents, Beppy Bruzzone, the long-serving secretary of the Italian Class and Marc Guichard (FRA) were elected. Continuity was provided by treasurer Jes Retbøll.

Also in 1985 Eric Hansen retired as chairman of the Technical Committee but remained as an International Measurer. He was succeeded by John Boorman of Canada but communications again proved a problem and in 1988 he too was succeeded by another Dane, Jens Andersen. That committee was strengthened by the addition of Fred Kats from the Netherlands and, two years later, Patrick Bergmans, a professor at Ghent University in Belgium. On the Regatta Committee Michel Barbier continued to upgrade the quality of racing at the Worlds and in 1985 was joined by René Kluin. Both were later to serve as Olympic Race Officers.

These were busy times for IODA. 1983 was in many ways the year in which IODA established the features which were to set the framework for future development. The major developments of a European Championship and team racing at the Worlds are described below. 1983 also saw the first IODA Yearbook, financed by the Junior Sailing Squadron of Thailand and printed there under the supervision of Nancy Chandler. Interestingly the main advertisement was for the Laser Radial, recently developed by Performance Sailcraft, an indication of the importance of the Optimist to the growth of youth sailing. 1983 also saw the start of the practice of collecting data about sailors at the Worlds, the 'Skipper Questionnaires', analysis of which provided a unique insight into the *facts* about the top sailors. This was to prove invaluable in explaining Class activity to outsiders, to say nothing of their value in writing this history.

European Championship

A recurrent theme in the 1980 reports from National Class Associations had been the need for a new level of international regatta. As the Germans put it: *"We think that there is a big gap between our national regattas and the World Championship."* Scandinavia and the Balkans already had regional events but in Europe the 'West European Championship' in Carantec, created when the 1973 Worlds in Rhodesia had had to be cancelled, was not regarded as an official event and did not rotate between different countries.

The need for a true European Championship was increased by the 1983 and 1984 Worlds both being outside Europe and the first such championship was held in Spain in 1983. Seven sailors per country were allowed and from the start some countries did not send their first teams. For example world champion Jordi Calafat did not participate and the first winner was his compatriot Javier Garcia who was only 12 at the time. While sending different sailors does not seem to have become a rule until 1995, most countries used the new event to increase the total number of sailors selected for national teams.

Records of the first event in 1983 have not survived but in 1984 in Genoa 81 sailors participated. By 1986 this had grown to 130 sailors and in the latter part of the decade numbers grew dramatically due to the increasing number of East European teams, the increase in 1987 in national quotas from seven to eight - in practice an extra girl - and the acceptance of non-European teams.

	1986	1990
"West European"	110	145
"East European"*	19	45	* Former Comecon & Yugoslavia
Non-European	1	28
	130	218
(Girls)	(33)	(74)

From 1986 places were reserved for two girls (increased to three the following year) who raced as a separate fleet. In that year 15 of the 18 countries present sent a total of 33 girls. This proved a momentous development, not least because at least seven of the 33 would go on to become Olympic sailors including fifth-placed Natalia Via Dufresne (ESP) who would take silver in the first ever women's single-handed event in 1992. By the end of the decade the number had more than doubled (68 European girls in 1990) and most members were sending their full quota of girls.

Until around 1993 this European Championship was in practice organised by a European group and the event sought little input from the IODA Regatta Committee. However from 1988 non-European teams were admitted and rising expectations of the quality of racing led to it being brought fully under democratic IODA control. The all-important choice of venue was in future made at the IODA AGM by the official representatives of the European countries.

European countries were now selecting 13 *different* sailors for official teams which opened up the team selection process. A number of future Olympic champions including, for example, Iain Percy in 1988-90, thereby gained the opportunity for truly international racing at an early age.

Team Racing

One of the first initiatives of the Regatta Committee created in 1982 was to introduce team racing for the Worlds of 1983 in Brasil. Previously the IODA Challenge Cup team prize had been awarded on the aggregate scores in the individual racing.

From the beginning Optimist team racing took place between teams of four rather than the conventional three. The reason was that countries sent five sailors to the Worlds and it was felt that it would be disruptive to leave two of the five ashore. With four-boat racing the fifth sailor could go afloat as reserve and might even sail in some of the matches. There were and remain objections from aficionados that this is not a pure form of the discipline but social considerations, as so often in the Optimist Class, prevailed.

In 1983 three days were allocated for team racing and at that first event a pool system for 17 teams required 70 races. However from 1991 at latest the event was reduced to the top 16 teams and the pool system was replaced by direct elimination with repechage (borrowed from the sport of fencing). This reduced the event to 30 races, sailed on only one day plus, if needed, part of the rest day. Around the same time teams were seeded on the results of the first days of fleet racing rather than previous year's results.

Initially protests arising from racing were heard ashore which could lead to late night hearings and, disastrously, a wasted day to hear over 100 protests in Helsinki in 1985. Direct judging (or umpiring as it came to be known) was only introduced in 1988. The IYRU had held a judges symposium in 1987 and minuted: *"Refereeing (giving decisions during racing) match and team racing is an important development within the sport"* and it *"hopes organising authorities experiment . . . during 1988"*.

The French FFV were quick to follow this up and in November 1987 organised a *Coupe de France* for team racing in several Classes, including the Optimist, with what they termed "direct judging on request" (*arbitrage direct solicité*). They came down strongly in favour of voluntary 360° turns with 720°

turns imposed by the judges where infringements were not acknowledged. A similar experiment was conducted at the ASEAN Optimist championship in Thailand. Following these experiments (and alternatives such as holding protest hearings on the committee boat after each race) IODA adopted the new system in the following year.

GRP: the ongoing saga

In 1982-3 IODA 'grasped the nettle' of the diversity of types of GRP Optimists which had been identified by Viggo and his colleagues on their visits to boat shows in the late 70s.

In December 1982 IODA issued a paper:

" *As recently as six months ago we were still encumbered with the perennial problems of the GRP hull. Since the introduction of the fibreglass boat in 1969, the GRP 'design' has gone through a lengthy development process which had produced a far better boat than the one we started out with. At the same time, though, there have been more or less continuous difficulties with manufacturers' interpretations of the GRP supplementary drawings, so that, despite a very considerable effort on the part of the Technical Committee, there have been many unresolved problems. It now looks as if the corner has been turned.*"

" *The Technical Committee has chosen* **a single-walled hull** *with a double bottom for the new One Design. The aim is to have the draft plan ready for distribution to member countries in the spring, and to have a prototype in Rio de Janeiro in July* [1983].*"

The background to this decision was threefold.

Firstly, for three years, following the findings of the Boat Show visits noted above, IODA and the IYRU had been receiving drawings and measurement forms from GRP builders seeking a 'Certificate of General Approval of Construction'. These had clearly shown the "difficulties with manufacturers' interpretations".

The second influence was that the Worlds of 1981 had shown that the Winner Optimist in particular was at least as fast as the best wooden boats. Not only had double world champion Johan Petterson been relegated, albeit narrowly, to second place by the Winner of Guido Tavelli (ARG) but at least five of the top ten had sailed that boat. In 1982 Njall Sletten (NOR) also won in a Winner. And the Winner had a single-walled hull.

The third factor was the desire to move or restore the Class to being one-design. Al Chandler issued a paper which accompanied the notice quoted above in which he outlined the reasons:

" *The Optimist dinghy is not at present a strict one design class.*" " *The Optimist class is at present neither strictly 'one design' nor 'development'. It originally was a 'home built' class in wood, with tolerances wide enough to allow building errors. Along came amateurs and professionals who used these tolerances to develop improved hull design, and, combined with the introduction of GRP and new building techniques, this has been very beneficial to the class.*"

But:

" *Rich national associations can afford both to purchase top quality boats and to transport them anywhere in the world. Skippers from poorer class associations and distant class associations are discriminated against.*"

" *One needs to identify overall policy objectives and decide on priorities. One objective of IODA is to promote fair and enjoyable sailing for young people of all nationalities. A second major objective is to encourage a high standard of competitive sailing skills.*"

The market did not wait for the prototype promised for Rio in July 1983, nor even for the results of the 1981 Worlds. In Germany for example at the 1980 Nationals there had been one single Winner: the following year 54% of participants sailed them.

The Winner Optimist developed by Henning Wind, bronze medallist in the Finn Class at the 1964 Olympics, was an excellent boat. The concept was to use buoyancy bags which were the most reliable form of buoyancy and to place them within what *looked* like the buoyancy tanks used on most Olympic boats but, by allowing drainage at the bottom, were not the 'empty cavities' rightly rejected by the

IODA Technical Committee. Single-wall construction reduced the likelihood of concentrating weight within double-walled construction. Finally the hull shape chosen proved to be highly efficient.

Understandably many builders, especially Falsled, had been unhappy at the decision to standardise on a single-walled hull and an attempt was made at the 1983 IODA AGM to reject the Technical Committee's proposal and continue to allow double-walled construction, but it was rejected by 9 votes to 7 with 8 abstentions. In November 1984 the IYRU approved the new rules, though building to older plans and rules was permitted until 1 January 1986.

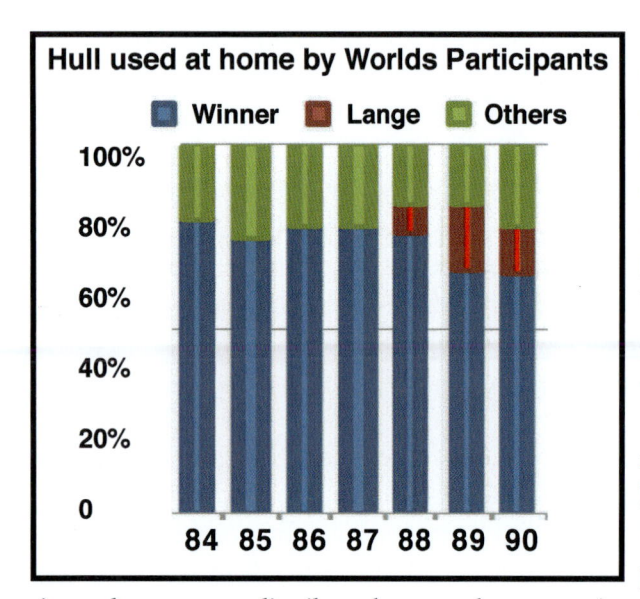

Hull used at home by Worlds Participants

■ Winner ■ Lange ■ Others

By the time global statistics were available from the 'Skipper Questionnaires' in 1984, 80% of sailors at the Worlds were qualifying for their national teams using Winners and this pattern continued for the next three years. By 1988 this dominance was being diluted by the arrival of the Lange Optimist from Argentina (at the 1990 Worlds 65% of sailors had qualified in Winners, 13% in Langes) but there was no other serious challenger for share of this market in the decade.

It was never clear what proportion of the *total* market Winner and Lange achieved. In Great Britain 65% of *all* GRP Optimists sold in 1982-1990 were Winners. In 1990 55% of *all* IYRU plaques sold were to Denmark or Argentina but, since plaques were distributed to member countries not builders, it is not certain who were the builders in those countries.

Changing times: a Winner leads a Falsled which leads a wooden boat

The new decade was, however, to bring new challenges and opportunities in the development of a true one-design Optimist.

An 'Optimist Training Boat'?

In November 1988 the IYRU received a proposal directly from the British RYA "to introduce polyethylene plastic Optimists and broaden the rules regarding sandwich construction". The decision was rightly referred for consideration by IODA. By the following May the IYRU knew that IODA was unwilling to return to the free-for-all situation of the late 1970s but had got the impression, rightly or wrongly, that the IODA Executive were prepared to consider incorporating within the Class an 'Optimist Training Boat'.

Financially this was tempting, both for the IYRU (its share of plaque fees on *legal* Optimists was over 10% of the total plaque revenue from *all* Classes) and for IODA. But at the IODA AGM in Japan in October 1989 the idea to "give any form of recognition to 'training boats' which may look quite like Optimists but aren't." was firmly rejected. New president Helen Mary, supported by IODA vice-president Ng Ser Miang who was also now a member of the IYRU Permanent Committee (Council), presented a strong case that November and the two key IYRU committees, the CBC and CPOC, supported and even, as minuted, "applauded" the stand of the Class.

Spars

In the early 1980s there were some radical improvements to the spars and rig. These were suggested by Fred Kats from Rotterdam. One of the world's leading experts on antique clocks, he had a deep understanding of the mechanics involved. His first innovation was a pin on the forward side of the mast to hold a simple line to the boom and, by providing a counter-force to the vang, improved efficiency at the goose-neck.

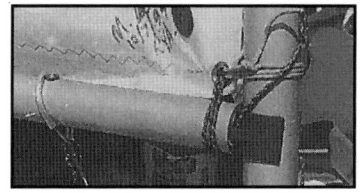

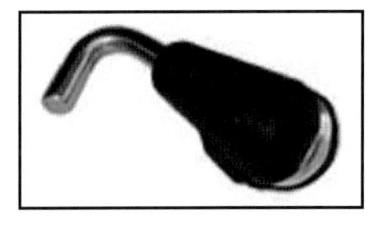

His second innovation is known as the Optimax system due to Fred's idea being produced by Bob Binnenweg who established the company of that name. The system solved the problem of having to remove the sail from the mast for overnight storage (and having to re-tie lots of knots in the morning) by having a removable sprit uphaul hook and wind indicator fitting.

A firm believer in the Class principle that 'anyone may build', Fred made his ideas available to all and they cost next to nothing. One major spar-maker developed an alternative system and briefly tried to persuade the IYRU to rule the Optimax system illegal and their alternative legal, claiming that IODA had granted a monopoly. Just why anyone would want a monopoly on a system which, even today, costs under $40 retail and can be made by any handyman, was never explained. The system was in fact probably cheaper than the earlier toothed rack.

What no-one could contest was the improvement in the quality of the aluminium used in the spars, introduced by Bob and rapidly emulated by others. While fairly expensive, these new spars were virtually indestructible, unlike those in many manufacturer-controlled Classes.

Fred, who was also a long-term member of the IYRU Centreboard Boat Committee, was, much later, to be a key figure in the specification of the 'IOD95' hull.

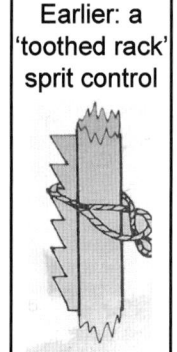

Earlier: a 'toothed rack' sprit control

The rise of specialist sailmakers

In the 1980s sailmaking became much more specialised - and an area of hot competition between sailmakers. No information is available for earlier years but as late as 1983 almost 80% of the sailors at the Worlds used sails made either by a large number of small sailmakers or the various North Sails lofts around the world.

Thereafter Optimist sailmaking at the top level became a specialised and, as can be seen below, a highly competitive industry. In vain the IODA Yearbook pointed out in 1985 and 1987 that the top ten sailors used sails from five different sailmakers. If your child was on the national team you *had* to buy whatever make of sail was fashionable that year. One of the reasons for the decline of smaller sailmakers may have been the increased specialisation of the sailcloth, with fewer manufacturers and larger minimum order quantities. Whatever the reason, the market has continued to swing between large manufacturers. However even in 2007 over twenty sailmakers worldwide each bought at least 50 sail-buttons a year and sailmakers such as David Mas in Catalonia are well-known for making small quantities of excellent sails.

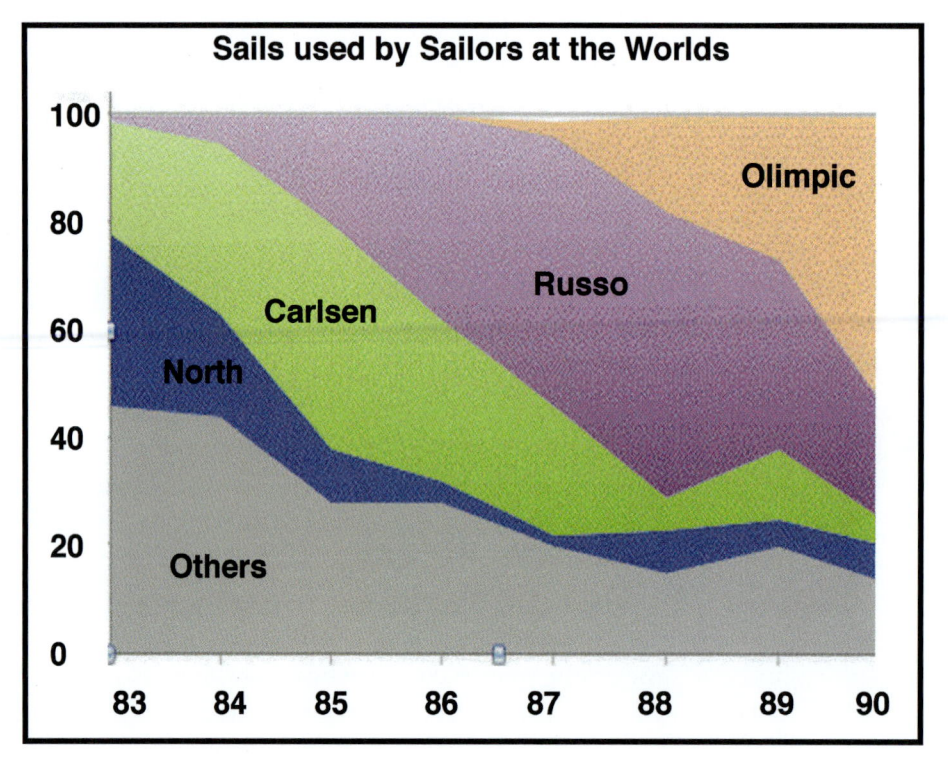

Regattas of the 1980s

With increasingly standardised equipment and rapidly expanding fleets elsewhere, the Scandinavian domination of the Worlds came to an end. Eleven nations supplied medallists during the decade. Spain was the most successful, initially with sailors from Mallorca - Jordi Calafat, José Carlos Frau and Nuria Bover - but later from many parts of Spain, due not least to RFEV subsidies for boats. Jordi reported that his boat cost 70,000 pesetas (USD470) but the federation had contributed 20,000 to it.

Specialist coaches began to appear. In 1981 observers were surprised to see that the coach to the Argentinian team was a 20-year old Santiago Lange. Most other teams were coached by parents; indeed not until later were coaches officially recognised as separate from team-leaders.

Venue		Individual		Best girl		Team*
1980	POR	Johan Petterson	SWE	Silvia Depares	ESP	DEN
		Rasmus Damsgaard	DEN			
		Marko Heiskanen	FIN			
1981	IRL	Guido Tavelli	ARG	Denise Lyttle	IRL	ARG
		Johan Petterson	SWE			
		Edson M Araujo	BRA			
1982	ITA	Njaal Sletten	NOR	Florence Rigolot	FRA	ESP
		Christian Rasmussen	DEN			
		Soren Ebdrup	DEN			
1983	BRA	Jordi Calafat	ESP	Florence Rigolot	FRA	FRA
		Jose Carlos Frau	ESP			
		Jean-Pierre Becquet	FRA			
1984	CAN	Serge Kats	NED	Veronique Ravet	FRA	DEN
		Jussi Wikström	FIN			
		Xavier Garcia	ESP			
1985	FIN	Serge Kats	NED	Nuria Bover	ESP	SWE
		Risto Tapper	FIN			
		Martin Castrillo	ARG			
1986	ESP	Xavier Garcia	ESP	Isobel Hens	BEL	FRA
		Luis Martinez D.	ESP			
		Risto Tapper	FIN			
1987	NED	Sabrina Landi	ITA	Sabrina Landi	ITA	ESP
		Luis Martinez D.	ESP			
		Anders Jonsson	SWE			
1988	FRA	Ugo Vanello	ITA	Maria Mylona	GRE	ESP
		Luis Martinez D.	ESP			
		Gabriel Tarrasa	ESP			
1989	JPN	Peder Rønholt	DEN	Suzanne Ward	DEN	DEN
		Rami Koskinen	FIN			
		Herman Rosso	ARG			

* From 1983 awarded for team-racing.

Ireland was the chosen venue only because Norway withdrew, and Howth, on the north side of Dublin Bay, was selected mostly due to the enthusiasm of Bill Lacy who was to serve on IODA juries for many years.

Light winds and strong tides curtailed the event. Johan Petterson (SWE) narrowly failed to become the only sailor to win three successive Worlds, losing out to Guido Tavelli (ARG). The Argentinian team was coached by the youthful Santiago Lange, a future Olympic medallist who may just have been looking at the new Winner Optimists.

Local spirits were raised by having an Irish girl, Denise Lyttle, first of the five girls present - a special trophy was hurriedly bought - and 14th over-all. Both she and Bettina Lemström (FIN) were future Olympians.

Helen Mary Wilkes was the Regatta Secretary and husband Robert the scorekeeper. After the final race one sailor was retrospectively disqualified from all races which, under the then Racing Rules, meant that *all* sailors had to be re-scored for *all* races. With the technology of the time this was an all-night job and results were finalised just before the prizegiving. That Racing Rule was changed shortly afterwards.

1982 FOLLONICA, ITALY   129 SAILORS FROM 26 COUNTRIES

The shoreside pine forest was a beautiful destination but the organisation was less than perfect. This was the period when international juries were beginning to observe racing but no one had thought to provide them with suitable boats.

Accommodation was in dormitories for 10-15 people. All the girls were in one dormitory but felt isolated from their teams and several moved back in with the boys. No doubt these days there are laws against that.

The winner was the hugely popular Njäl Sletten from Bergen in Norway, probably the northernmost champion ever. Despite a later skiing accident he was to have a long and distinguished sailing career and as of 2011 is tactician on the Royal Norwegian's Swan 42 *Bandit*.

1983 RIO DE JANEIRO, BRASIL   98 SAILORS FROM 22 COUNTRIES

For the first time the championship was held in South America and, while there were fewer European countries present, Chile and Venezuela brought the number of South American countries to five. The venue was the magnificent Iate Club do Rio de Janeiro based on hangars once used for flying boats.

For the first time ever GRP charter boats were mandatory, produced in Brasil from moulds supplied by Vanguard Boats of Newport, Rhode Island. The experiment was not an unqualified success since late entries and perhaps production delays led to insufficient boats.

However nothing could have stopped Jorge (later Jordi) Calafat of Spain, one of the most convincing winners ever with five victories in seven races. He remains the only Optimist Worlds gold medallist to win Olympic gold and in 2003 was strategist on America's Cup winners *Alinghi*. Two other 1983 participants also became Olympic champions. Thomas Johanson (FIN) won the first 49er gold in 2000 and Freddie Lööf (SWE) competed in *six* Olympics, gaining two bronzes in the Finn and Star Classes before finally winning gold in the Star in 2012.
France won the first ever team-racing championship, a reward for the pioneering work of the FFV in this discipline.

1984 KINGSTON, CANADA   132 SAILORS FROM 28 COUNTRIES

The venue was the Olympic site from 1976, now being run as a commercial company, and behind the scenes there were financial and other problems.

Among the sailors entered was a Polish team, the first ever entry from behind the then apparently solid 'iron curtain', which included Tomasz Chamera, later to be one of the world's leading race officers. Present too was Philippe Rogge, future Finn world champion and son of the future IOC president, together with his sister Caroline.

The championship was won by Serge Kats (NED) who was to win also in 1985 before a distinguished career in Lasers which included a heart-breaking 4th in the 2000 Olympics. His father Fred was to be a vital technical innovator for the Class, much involved with the 'IOD95' project.

Glasnost, the change in Soviet policy towards openness, is normally dated to 1986. If so then the Optimists may have got there first. Perhaps because the Worlds had returned to Europe, not only did the Poles attend again but so did teams from Bulgaria, Hungary and Yugoslavia. Probably coincidentally, there was present the first ever sailor, Yang Wu, from the closed world of China. As a result the number of countries present topped 30 for the first time.

On the water a major development was the birth of the idea that boats driven by national coaches would in future provide the main rescue function. The naval personnel provided by the organisers to tow the fleet to and from the course had decided that slalom routes swinging their tail of boats wildly behind them was rather fun.

Of perhaps even greater importance was the first appearance, at least in small sizes, of dry-suits. Over the next few years they would do much to extend the sailing season in colder climates.

Serge Kats won his second world championship.

Strong winds are the norm in the northern part of what we were learning to call Catalunya (some of the organisers still called the venue Rosas) and there were some wild races.

Perhaps for the only time in the history of the Worlds some sailors had to be rescued by local in-

shore fishing boats. Correctly these took the sailors aboard and left the boats until later. All the Optimists were in fact retrieved safely as they wallowed full of water; thereafter there was less talk of the virtues of self-draining systems.

The winner was Javier Garcia Muret from the nearby club of El Balís who had taken bronze in Canada in 1984 and fourth place in 1985. At 1m75 and 60 kg he clearly revelled in the conditions. Among the other participants was the great Robert Scheidt (four Olympic medals) but even at the age of 13 he was already almost as big as Javier and rightly left the Class shortly thereafter.

Another future great sailor was present under rather strange circumstances. Xavier Revil, most recently a helmsman on *Banque Populaire V*, holders of the Jules Verne Trophy, was entered for Senegal. There was a strong suspicion at the time that this was a second French team in disguise, but his official biography confirms that he was indeed resident there.

For the first time in the history of the Worlds, after 25 years, IODA had a female champion in Sabrina Landi of Italy.

The previous year there had been a big debate as to whether IODA needed a separate girls' world championship, splitting the fleet as was now the practice at the Europeans. Many coaches were in favour but the female sailors were adamant: they were as good as the boys and wanted the chance to prove it. Now Sabrina had done so.

An amusing side issue was the weighing of clothing. In this period the IYRU was battling against weight jackets and a few coaches had the not-too-clever idea that if one wore a heavy sweater under the new dry-suits and let in a little water this would produce the same effect. So it was necessary to conduct weighing of clothing. This required sailors to strip to their under-garments but no one had foreseen that girls would be involved. Fortunately Helen Mary was available to help.

The venue in Holland brought to prominence René Kluin, one of the first to qualify as an IYRU International Race Officer. He devoted many years to improving race management in the Optimist and was to become IODA's fifth president.

1988 LA ROCHELLE, FRANCE   145 SAILORS FROM 32 COUNTRIES

The famous venue produced a new record turnout including for the first time sailors from Singapore. The event was won by Ugo Vanelo from La Spezia, Italy, with Luis Martinez Doreste of the great Gran Canaria sailing dynasty taking his third successive silver. A French reporter at the time claimed that Ugo was boxed in by the strong Spanish team: this seems unlikely since he scored 1, 2 and 3 in the final races of the series.

The dominance of the Winner Optimist reached its peak. In La Rochelle 82% of all participants sailed Winners and 9% - the South Americans plus Spain - sailed Langes, apparently specially shipped across the Atlantic for the event. The concept of the Optimist that "anyone may build" seemed to be slipping away.

1989 YOKOHAMA, JAPAN
126 SAILORS FROM 30 COUNTRIES

The decision to return to an Asian venue after ten years proved a great success in attracting seven Asian countries - China, Indonesia, Japan, Korea, Singapore, Malaysia and Thailand, and the first ever Oceanian entry from Tahiti.

Meticulous planning by Dr. Ben Majima, the father of the Japanese fleet, raised to new heights the standard of the shore venue at a newly developed unused fishing harbour.

Racing took place on the fringe of a typhoon and gave spectacular conditions relished by the winner Peder Rønholt (DEN) who, at 1m83 and 59kg remains the tallest victor in the history of the event. Both he and girls' winner Susanne Ward (on the right of the photo) went on to take part in the Olympics.

A highlight was the presence of Princess Takamodo who managed to step off the storm-ridden spectator boat looking as if she had just left a beauty salon.

Taking the Worlds to Japan (and possibly the presence of royalty) produced exceptional growth there, from 366 sailors in 1988 to 949 in 1992, at least 300 of these in state-sponsored sailing schools.

Continental Championships

The origin and growth of the European championship has been described above. Results were as follows:

Venue		Boys		Girls	
1983	ESP	Javier Garcia	ESP		
1984	ITA	Javier Garcia	ESP		
1985	FRA	Paul Maxime	FRA		
1986	AUT	Vesa Kukkonen	FIN	Laura Leon	ESP
1987	GRE	Mario Noto	ITA	Federica Prunai	ITA
1988	HUN	Aless. Bonifacio	ITA	Antonia Campos	ITA
1989	SWE	Martin Nielsen	SWE	Susanne Ward	DEN

The South American Championship created in 1973 had expanded from its three nation circuit in the mid-1980s to include Chile (hosts in 1985) and Peru (hosts in 1989 - future IODA president Peter Barclay was the PRO). Venezuela participated intermittently and by 1989 Ecuador also attended.

	Venue	Champion			Venue	Champion	
1980	ARG	Carlos Wanderley	BRA	1985	CHI	Ricardo Tramujas	BRA
1981	URU	Carlos Wanderley	BRA	1986	BRA	Ricardo Tramujas	BRA
1882	BRA	Miguel Saubidet	ARG	1987	ARG	Cristobal Saubidet	ARG
1983	ARG	Miguel Saubidet	ARG	1988	URU	Manuel Miranda	ARG
1984	URU	A. Barbosa da Silva	BRA	1989	PER	Francisco Paillot	ARG

Above are 'closed' champions. The outright winner in 1987 & 8 was Mark Mendelblatt (USA).

The North American Championship had been created in 1976, but with no fleet in Mexico until 1987 and the (temporary) decline of Optimist sailing in Bermuda, the championship had become in practice a USA event with, usually, a small team from Canada and a few visitors from South America. Again results sheets are not available before 1989 but three of the known winners were from St. Petersburg: David and Mark Mendelblatt and Ed Sherman (1989). All winners of the US Nationals, for which results *are* available, were from Florida (St. Pete, Coconut Grove and Coral Reef). Girls occasionally made the US team, notably Kim Logan in 1985 and Mandy Bremen in 1989.

A curiosity was the appearance in 1989 of a team from the French territory of St. Pierre et Miquelon (at 46°47' N).

While there was an ASEAN (South East Asian) Championship from 1987, the first Asian Championship was just after the end on the decade in 1990.

Growth in the 1980s

Geographical expansion of the Optimists was less spectacular than in the previous decade. While IODA acquired at least twelve new members, most of the new fleets were, for the time being, small:

1981	Angola, Chinese Taipei
1984	China
1985	Malta
1986	San Marino, Tunisia,
1987	Ecuador, Mexico
1989	Andorra, DDR (East Germany), Malaysia, Tahiti

Angola participated in the 1981 & 83 Worlds

Chapter 5: the 1990s

Al Chandler retired in 1989 having achieved a radical modernisation of the Class. IODA was now firmly established in Asia (Japan was the venue for the 1989 Worlds) and had a prestigious Yearbook, a proper Constitution and a set of Conditions for the World Sailing Championship. With around 60 member countries on all six continents, more than half of them attending the Worlds, and three growing continental championships, IODA had truly progressed.

The new president was Helen Mary Wilkes who had already seven years of experience on IODA committees. Elected as a vice-president was Ng Ser Miang from Singapore, the first Asian member

Helen Mary with Viggo & Edith

of the Executive, who was to have a big impact on Asian sailing and was to go on to become a vice-president of the International Olympic Committee. Continuity was provided by Jes Retbøll as the other vice president. Engineering professor Patrick Bergmans became chairman of the Technical Committee and future IODA president René Kluin joined the Executive the following year as chair of the Regatta Committee

IODA's finances were in a poor state with reserves equal to just three months normal expenses. Treasurer Aad Offermans (NED) bluntly stated that, unless IODA wished to be controlled only by those who could afford to finance it, additional income must be found. The AGM agreed to introduce a sail button at a cost of $5 for each sail sold. It was agreed that at least $1 of this would be allocated to training.

An immediate innovation was the Optiworld newsletter. Produced and initially sponsored by Robert, it replaced the typed 'Information' sheets which had been started by Al and contained articles of general interest as well as notices of race, rule changes, the official calendar and other administrative information. Since, from the second issue in March 1990, it contained advertising by suppliers, it soon produced enough revenue to pay the postal costs to all members.

Administration in the 1990s

One of the immediate concerns of the new Executive was to limit the personal financial liability of the committee members and others undertaking work for IODA, and to ensure that it was accepted as a not-for-profit organisation. After extensive study of laws and company structures in various countries, it emerged that Danish law offered the best solution to these two objectives and in 1993 IODA was formally registered as an 'Institution of Public Utility' in Denmark. It was a tribute to Al's legal expertise that his Constitution required only minor changes to become the 'Articles of Association' of the new company.

Patrick retired in 1992 but as a member of the IYRU/ISAF Council has continued to keep an unofficial advisory role. In the same year Jes Retbøll also retired after long service. His place was taken by Norman Jenkins from Argentina, another successful businessman and experienced offshore sailor whose son, now out of the Class, had won two Worlds. When Ser Miang retired to become a vice-president of the IYRU he was succeeded by Gudrun von Dahl (1993-1997) and then Mimi Santos, both highly competent national Class secretaries. IODA did not always have a separate treasurer but following the sad death of John Meade (USA) the position was occupied by Roland Tan from Malaysia who had the great advantage of representing IODA to the fast-growing Asian members.

Technical matters, including the critical development of the IOD95, were heavily influenced by Fred Kats but he steadily refused to either chair the committee or to become a measurer. The more phlegmatic Dominique Langlois (FRA) oversaw the critical period but the task of maintaining technical standards then passed to Curly Morris from Northern Ireland and Hans Thijsse from South Africa who successively chaired the committee. The number of qualified International Measurers increased to seven by the end of the decade.

The regatta committee was throughout in the highly capable hands of close friends René Kluin and Michel Barbier, who had been among the very earliest International Race Officers when that ISAF qualification was introduced in 1989. No specialist in shore organisation was appointed as Helen Mary continued to do much of this job herself with the help of a more active group of vice-presidents.

Change of secretariat

The workload on the secretariat in Århus had been greatly increased by the need to administer the 'IOD95' (See chapter 6; around 3,300 Registration Books would be issued in the year) and the communications resulting from e-mail. In mid-1996 Hanne Rix advised that she wished to retire as secretary of IODA. It was the end of an era since Hanne had been associated with IODA for a quarter of a century with outstanding dedication and loyalty.

Robert Wilkes had long been 'working' for IODA, having created the *Optiworld* newsletter in 1989, produced the Yearbook from 1991, created the website in 1995, and already taken on much of the increase in general workload. Having retired from his business in 1995 he now volunteered to run the secretariat. People retiring early are often advised to turn their hobbies into a business and IODA, with a turnover now five times that of ten years previously, needed to be turned into an efficient business and to take full advantage of the new internet technology.

Wider and wider

The 1990s saw much faster growth in member countries, from 60 to 97, though this did include seven newly independent nations. New members came primarily from three specific regions.

In Asia Ng Ser Miang was immediately into action to expand on the interest created by the 1989 Worlds in Japan. At the first IODA Asian Championship held in December 1990, Singapore welcomed nine Asian countries including five - India, Hong Kong, Myanmar, Pakistan and the Philippines - which had not been present at the Worlds. The following year he negotiated to take the event to Qingdao, perhaps the first major sailing event in that city.

This event in China showed the advantages of the Optimist's 'free construction - anyone may build' principle. There was no way that the China of 1991 could import boats, so 50 Optimists were

constructed by a single family. Small business was not then permitted so they traded as the Qingdao Zou Sailing Club. These were probably the first boats produced in China for any ISAF Class and twenty years later what is now Zou Inter Marine is a major builder of Optimists. This freedom to encourage local manufacture was to be important also elsewhere in Asia, with builders becoming established also in Singapore and India. Ser Miang also ensured that Optimists were included in the Asian Games, Asian Sailing Championship and SEA Games: sports ministries did not have to be convinced that the Optimist was the pathway to these prestige events and beyond.

Also in 1990 Eastern Europe became the next focus for IODA following the break-up of Soviet domination. Czechoslovakia and Hungary had participated in the Europeans at least as early as 1986 and when the event was held in Hungary in 1988, Poland and the USSR also participated. The 'USSR' tended in fact to be a team from Estonia and they were determined to travel. At the Europeans of 1990 in Denmark the hammer & sickle of the USSR went up at the opening ceremony: the following day the loudspeakers demanded the return of the stolen flag. The tricolour of Estonia occupied the flag-pole for the rest of the event. In the convoluted politics of that year the Estonians also turned up at Ser Miang's Asians, now competing as the 'Confederated States'. Tensions were high: a now forgotten novel by Warwick Collins even featured the Russians shooting at the fictional Estonian helm of an America's Cup yacht. Which did not prevent IODA president Helen Mary taking a short holiday in Tallinn that summer . . .

Following the break-up of the Soviet Union, IODA acquired five new members from its component parts. The changeover from state-sponsored sport was not easy and a number of top-level coaches chose to emigrate, including notably Victor Kovalenko (UKR), the 'medal-maker' who was to become the Australian national coach and much later partly responsible for the acceptance of the Optimist in that country. Participation in IODA events slowly increased and in 1995 Maxim Pidgurskiy (UKR) from the Black Sea won the Europeans to demonstrate that the USSR sailing tradition had not been confined to the Baltic.

The break-up of Yugoslavia was much more distressing - and stressful for IODA. The 1991 IODA European Championship had been allocated to Pula in what is now Croatia. In May IODA received a letter of reassurance from its mayor and issued a circular to members pointing out that "no European government is known to have advised its nationals not to visit this part of Yugoslavia". However the feeling of the European meeting at the Worlds was nervous and Pula finally withdrew. Fortunately the deposits had been lodged in an Italian bank and Vlado Barbic, soon to be the Class secretary in Croatia, ensured their return. The 1991 Europeans was finally held at Christmas at Anzio, Italy thanks to the untiring enthusiasm of Italian Class secretary Beppy Bruzzone. Attendance was down and there was little wind but at least we had a championship.

The third area of expansion was the Caribbean. This took place primarily in and after the latter part of the decade and will be described later.

New members 1990-1999:

1990	Paraguay, Hong Kong, Israel, Myanmar, Pakistan, Philippines. Seychelles, USSR/Russia
1991	Cyprus
1992	*Estonia*, Fiji, *Slovenia*
1993	Sri Lanka, *Slovakia*, Trinidad
1994	Antigua, Cayman, *Lithuania,*, Puerto Rico, USVI, *Ukraine*
1995	Guatemala, Luxembourg,
1996	*Belarus*, Egypt, Cook I., Kuwait
1997	British V.I., Kyrgyzstan, *Latvia*, Solomon I,
1999	Cuba, Qatar, U.A.Emirates

Note: Countries shown in italics resulted from political partition. Where a member country was divided the largest successor country is taken as the continuing member (e.g. Russia is considered as the 'heir' of the USSR). Others (e.g. *Ukraine*) are listed as new members.

Lift-off in the USA

The 1990s expansion in the USA was numerically even greater than the new fleets in the rest of the world put together.

It is hard to identify both why the Optimist was slow to develop in the USA through the 70s and 80s and why in 1989-90 it suddenly took off. A genuine North American Championship had been created in 1976 and there had been some expansion in 1979-82. In 1979 David Sinclair of the Noroton Y.C. in Darien, Connecticut, had bought 20 boats due to the influence of Nigel Ringrose. In 1980 John Lovell had introduced a further 20 to the Southern Y.C in New Orleans (his son was to become one of the USA's first ex-Optimist Olympic medallists) and a further 10 of the batch imported from Denmark had gone to the Fort Worth B.C. in Texas. In 1982 the Optimist had been adopted by the influential Severn Sailing Association in Annapolis which even imported a coach from Florida to raise standards.

However in 1988 USODA reported only around 350 members with only seven states having viable fleets and around 100 new sail numbers a year issued since 1984. In 1990 this suddenly jumped to nearly 600. The second ever *Optiworld* newsletter in March 1990 rejoiced that the Optimist had been adopted by the regional yachting associations of Minnesota/Wisconsin, Massachusetts and Long Island Sound (New York/Connecticut). Recognition followed from the Inland Lakes Yachting Association with new fleets in Illinois, Iowa and Ohio, and the number of states with serious fleets was estimated at 17.

This may have been a somewhat delayed consequence of the first expansion noted above. President of USODA at the time was the larger than life figure of John Meade from Louisiana (*"you know those levées: I keep them there"*). Under his influence USODA took major events to Marblehead, to Lake Michigan and to the great New York Yacht Club in Rhode Island, where reportedly the young sailors revelled in rolling down the bank of its hallowed lawns. John, who died tragically in a boating accident, was succeeded by Floridan Rick Bischoff but, very importantly, Joni Palmer from Annapolis became Executive Director (and a member of the IYRU Youth Committee). Other important figures were Bill Douglas as editor of the vital *Optinews* newsletter and secretary Ken Slater. Under their influence and that of such influential supporters as top I. J. Barbara Farquhar, new sail numbers rose still further, reaching nearly 1,000 a year in the latter part of the decade, and there were estimated to be fleets in 36 states.

The puzzle remains why it took so long for the Optimist to spread. There was no serious competition from an alternative junior single-hander except in California. On the supply side Laser builder Vanguard and several others had been producing acceptable Optimists throughout the 1980s, though top sailors tended to use imported Winners or Langes, as they did until McLaughlin, who started production in 1990, made some inroads towards the end of the decade with the growing belief in the 'IOD95'. It is tempting to think that the victory of ex-Optimist Allison Jolly, the only USA gold medallist in the 1988 Olympics, may have made the U.S. authorities look harder at the Class, and *American Sailor* magazine speculated that the loss of the America's Cup had caused some re-thinking. But a tentative conclusion must be that individuals do change history. If so then the lift-off may have been due to an outstanding group of individuals who showed what the descendent of Clark Mills' boat could do for junior sailing.

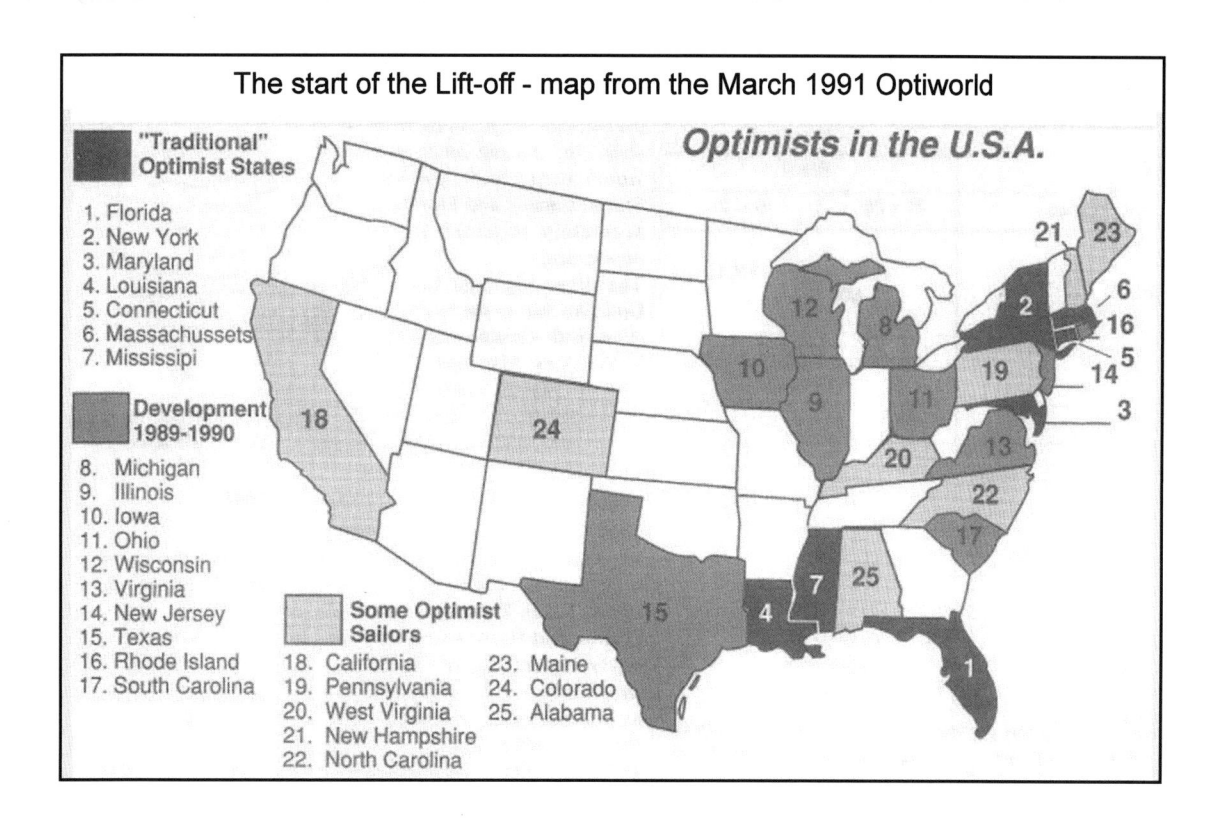

The start of the Lift-off - map from the March 1991 Optiworld

Optimists in the U.S.A.

"Traditional" Optimist States

1. Florida
2. New York
3. Maryland
4. Louisiana
5. Connecticut
6. Massachussets
7. Mississipi

Development 1989-1990

8. Michigan
9. Illinois
10. Iowa
11. Ohio
12. Wisconsin
13. Virginia
14. New Jersey
15. Texas
16. Rhode Island
17. South Carolina

Some Optimist Sailors

18. California
19. Pennsylvania
20. West Virginia
21. New Hampshire
22. North Carolina
23. Maine
24. Colorado
25. Alabama

Venues

The venues to which USODA took its Nationals in the 1990s tell their own story. Before 1990 all championships had been held in Florida.

1990	Grosse Point	Michigan	1995	Charleston	South Carolina
1991	Coral Reef	Florida	1996	Rochester	New York
1992	Newport	Rhode Island	1997	Gulfport	Mississipi
1993	Lake Geneva	Wisconsin	1998	Marblehead	Massachusets
1994	Houston	Texas	1999	Hampton	Virginia

The arrival of the internet

In 1994 IODA was an early user of the internet, accessing the first sailing forum on Compuserve. At the May 1995 IYRU meeting a presentation was made by Bernie Stegmeier, president of the Swiss Yachting Association and a director of IBM, and Robert made contact with David McCreary, former sailing coach of Cornell University, who was establishing the 'Sailing Source' to develop websites for the sport.

The costs of creating websites were high. The IYRU was quoted the 'bargain' fee of $30,000 but would not approve such expenditure; president Paul Henderson records that he personally engaged McCreary to create its first website. IODA certainly could not afford such fees but McCreary offered to host a site for IODA and explained how to create webpages by learning HTML (at that time version 2.0) code and borrowing shamelessly from the source code of any attractive site. Robert had recently retired from the printing industry and had the necessary hard- and software to do so.

The MkI IODA website, published in June 1995, was as shown. If it looks primitive, it was. HTML was far from standardised so different browsers 'saw' websites differently. Many dial-up modems worked at 28.8KB/s so file sizes had to be tiny. Pages themselves were 8 or 12 KB and graphics had to be in .GIF format, the largest of them being the Nesquik Bunny at 33KB.

However the first IODA website contained a lot of information:

- an introduction which included the information that beginners' boats started around $1,300
- the Class Rules, tortuously converted into HTML
- a list of the 60 member countries with *fax* or phone numbers
- a calendar of some 30 of the biggest regattas (but no contact details)
- headline news, with an invitation to subscribe to the *printed* Optiworld newsletter
- the results (top 10 only) of the IODA South Americans held that April.

What it did not contain was a link to the website of sponsors Nesquik, for the simple reason that Nestlé had no website! Primitive this first website may seem but it still won the award of Best Class Website when these awards were instituted by Henderson in November 1995.

It is amusing in retrospect to read what was published in the June 1995 Optiworld newsletter:

"The potential of the Internet, the 'information superhighway' for selling the Optimist Class and distributing information is becoming clear."
"Anyone in the world who is on the internet (there are 20 million already) can dial up and for a few pennies can get full details of the Class."

So far so good. However the article commented: *"The part of the Internet used for sending messages to people, E-mail, seems less useful so far . . . it is not possible to send documents that are not already on computer. You cannot for example send Sailing Instructions you received by mail to club members."* Scanners were rare and graphics files too big for the slow transmission.

This problem was solved a year later with the release of Adobe Acrobat 3.0. Dial-up modems were doubling their speed to 56k (5% of the speed of today's slowest broadband!) and the 20 million internet users had become over 100 million with, reportedly, traffic over the internet doubling every 100 days. By September 1999 it was realistic to upload the printed *Optiworld* newsletter, a vast improvement on mailing 10-15 copies per member country.

The internet was useful also for *collecting* information. For example IODA had long believed that many Olympic skippers were former Optimist sailors but only now was it possible to prove this by searching their internet data, in particular for birth-year, and checking this against (paper) Optimist results for the appropriate years. Being able to prove, in particular to newer sailing countries, that the Optimist was the normal starter boat of Olympians was a

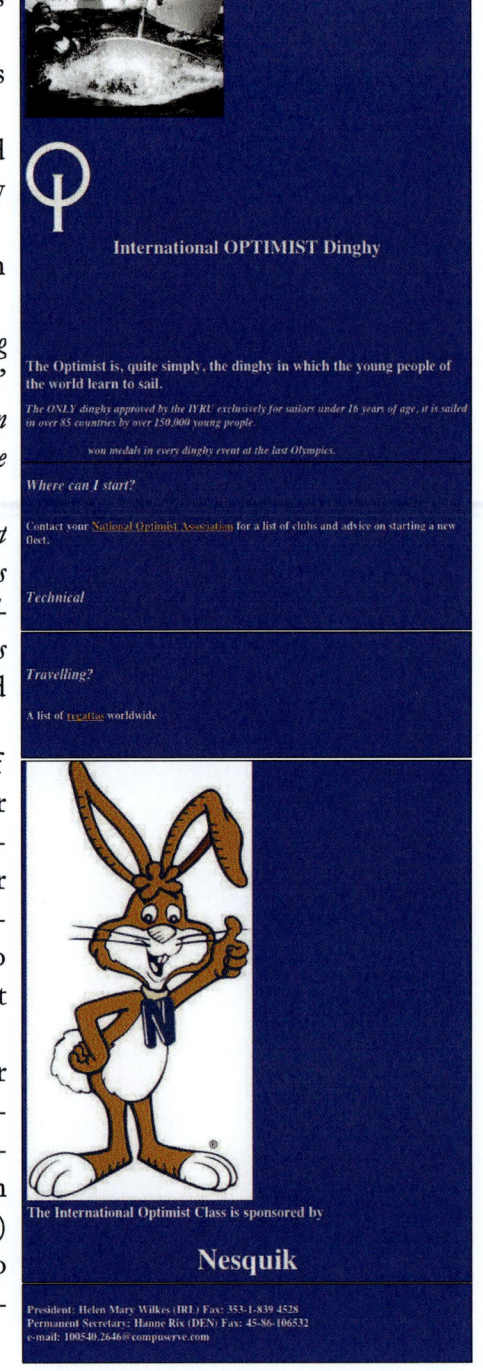

valuable tool in promoting the Class.

By the end of the decade the IODA website looked a lot prettier and was linked to a lot more information.

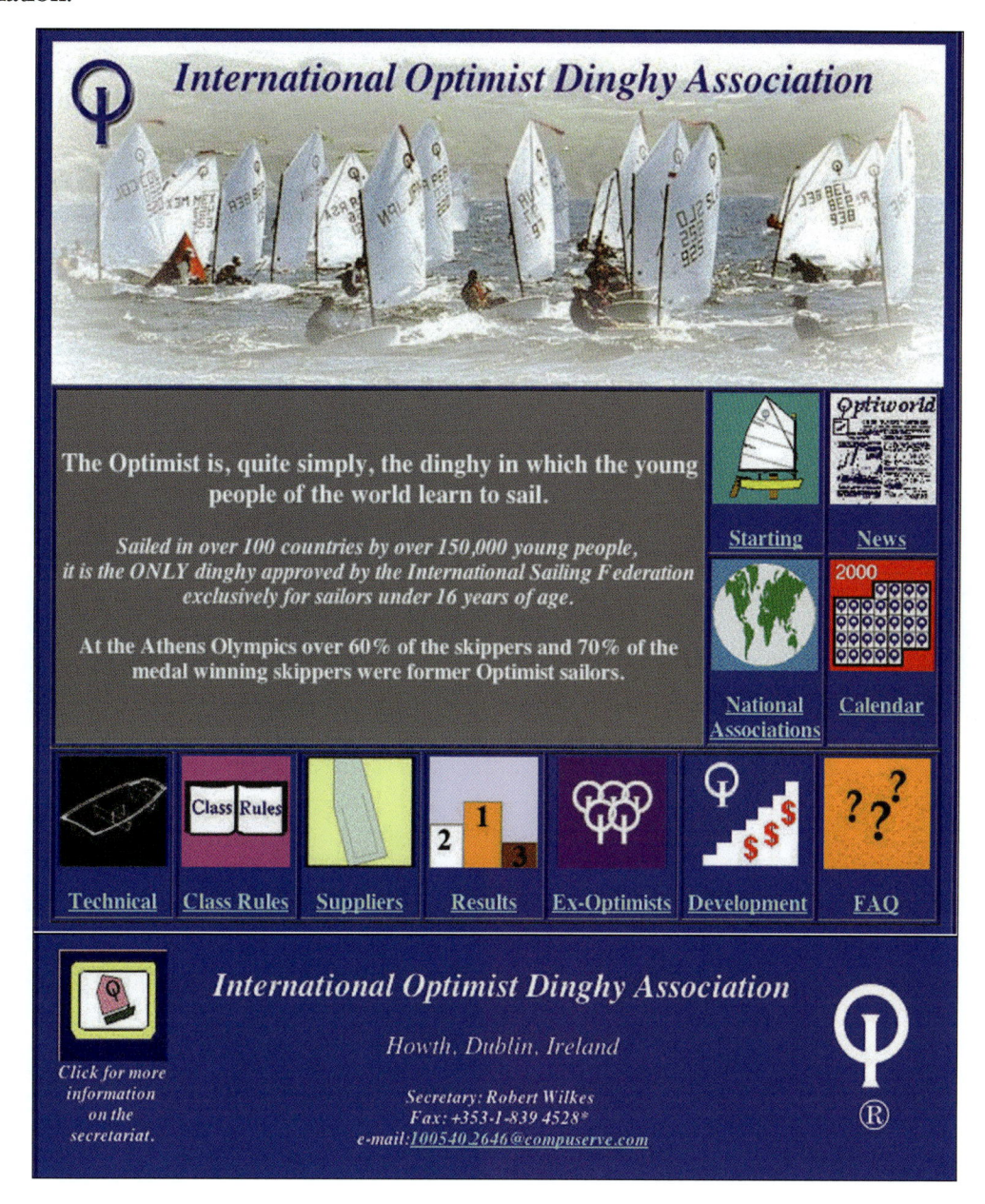

Nesquik sponsorship 1995 - 1997

For three years from 1995 to 1997 IODA enjoyed the benefits of some of the best sponsorship any dinghy Class ever experienced.

The origin was an introduction by Mme Yves Challand of the Swiss Optimist Association, followed by a successful presentation to the annual conference of Nestlé companies worldwide. The result was an arrangement whereby Nestlé would sponsor IODA's own development programme with US$40,000 a year and this would be enhanced by national sponsorship in certain countries where the national Nestlé company and the national Optimist association could reach agreement on local sponsorship.

The agreement was based on voluntary co-operation at national level and was more successful in some countries than others, depending on the local Nestlé and local Optimist people. The most successful local agreements were as follows:

Portugal: Mimi Santos, the long-serving secretary of the Portuguese O.D.A., quickly developed a programme whereby Nesquik promotions took place at a large number of local regattas all along the coast. Nesquik were major sponsors of the 1995 Europeans and, even after the formal agreement ended, of the 1998 Worlds.

South Africa: The country had already been awarded the 1996 IODA World Championship and Hans Thijsse, another long-serving Class officer, was delighted to negotiate Nesquik title sponsorship of the event. They also sponsored the 1995 and 1996 national championships.

Chile: Nesquik sponsored the 1995 South Americans in Algorrobo.

Greece: 500 suitably embroidered Nesquik buoyancy-aids were sponsored. Similar aids were also donated to all participants at the 1995 Worlds.

Smaller amounts were negotiated in Austria, New Zealand, Myanmar, Norway and Turkey.

Unfortunately the sponsorship was not renewed at the end of 1997. While the Nestlé HQ marketing manager Graeme Livingstone-Wallace assured IODA that Head Office had regarded the sponsorship as a success, it was financed by contributions from national Nestlé companies. Several of those which had initially shown interest had not done so at local level and Graeme was unable to persuade the necessary ten countries to continue with the project.

But Nesquik had sponsored two highly successful Worlds and two continental championships. More importantly the $120,000 which IODA had received over the three years had directly enabled it to expand its development program of courses in many newer countries (see chapter 10), to finance much of the 'IOD95' inspection programme, and to sponsor sailors at the 1999 and 2000 Worlds.

Regattas of the 1990s

World Championships

	Venue	Countries	Individual		Best girl		Team
1990	POR	38	Martín di Pinto	ARG	Natalie Gunst	BEL	ARG
			Agustin Krevisky	ARG			
			Martin Strandberg	SWE			
1991	GRE	39	Agustin Krevisky	ARG	Gaia Lusini	ITA	BRA
			Asdrubal Garcia	ARG			
			André Sørensen	DEN			
1992	ARG	29	Ramón Oliden	ARG	Claudia Tosi	ITA	ITA
			Marc Patiño	ESP			
			Mike Keser	GER			
1993	ESP	41	Mats Hellman	NED	Claudia Tosi	ITA	ARG
			Esteban Rocha	ARG			
			Claudia Tosi	ITA			
1994	ITA	39	Martín Jenkins	ARG	Johanna Saerna	SWE	ARG
			Federico Perez	ARG			
			Julio Alsogaray	ARG			
1995	FIN	41	Martín Jenkins	ARG	Lisa Westerhof	NED	ESP
			Frederico Rizzo	BRA			
			Dario Kliba	CRO			
1996	RSA	39	Lisa Westerhof	NED	Lisa Westerhof	NED	ARG
			Aron Lolic	CRO			
			Ivan Bertaglia	ITA			
1997	IRL	41	Luca Bursic	ITA	Siren Sundby	NOR	PER
			Matias Buhler	ARG			
			Nicholas Raygada	PER			
1998	POR	44	Mattia Pressich	ITA	Tina Celigoj	SLO	PER
			Fernando Gwozdz	ARG			
			Sime Fantela	CRO			
1999	FRA	**47**	Mattia Pressich	ITA	Roberta Borges	BRA	PER
			Tonci Stipanovic	CRO			
			Mario Coutinho	POR			

The Miami Herald

With the main team prize, the IODA Challenge Cup, now awarded for team racing, the Miami Herald Trophy was used for the combined team achievement (aggregate scores of four best results). It was a good indicator of the swinging fortunes of national teams. The leading nations in the 1990s were as follows:

1990	Spain	Sweden	Denmark	1996	Croatia	Brasil	Italy
1991	Italy	Spain	Yugoslavia	1997	Argentina	Italy	Denmark
1992	Argentina	Italy	Netherlands	1998	Argentina	Italy	Brasil
1993	Argentina	Brasil	Spain	1998	Argentina	Italy	Brasil
1994	Argentina	Denmark	Brasil	1999	Croatia	Peru	Portugal
1995	France	Brasil	Argentina				

1990 CASCAIS, PORTUGAL
173 SAILORS FROM 38 COUNTRIES

The return to Europe saw a quantum leap in participation, almost 20% higher than the record of the 1980s. Peru entered for the first time, Malaysia and Tahiti for the second, and the *Glasnost* effect brought teams from Bulgaria, Poland and Romania. Among the participants were 26 girls, more than

double the 1988 figure, among them Margriet Matthijsse (NED) who was to have the distinction of participating in the Olympics in both the single- and double-handed events, winning two silver medals in the former.

Winds were, initially at least, predominantly light and, with the whole fleet racing together - 173 boats on the same start line - the final race was exceptionally close. Martín di Pinto (ARG) was the eventual winner and Argentina also won the team-racing championship in what was to be the start of a decade of Argentinian dominance.

1991 PORTO CARRAS, GREECE
184 SAILORS FROM 39 COUNTRIES

With an even bigger entry the Regatta Committee split the fleet onto two separate race courses. The experiment was not an unqualified success as dying wind on one of the courses left half that fleet DNF. The fleet was then split into gold and silver divisions but the latter seemed determined to provoke endless general recalls.

There was a crisis when the local race officers refused to accept the Hellenic Y.A. PRO (whose exploits at the Olympics thirteen years later are detailed in Paul Henderson's autobiography). IODA vice-president Ng Ser Miang, CEO of the Singapore transport system, knew a bit about negotiating and a compromise was reached: the PRO would 'supervise' racing by travelling from one committee boat to the other . . . without ever boarding either of them.

1990 silver medallist Agustin Krevisky took gold and in 5th place was future Olympic medallist Gustavo Lima (POR). The event was notable in that a record 35 girls participated and two placed in the top ten, but this proved to be something of a false dawn and it would be another nine years before this number was matched.

1992 MAR DEL PLATA, ARGENTINA
133 SAILORS FROM 29 COUNTRIES

Described at the time as the 'Happy Christmas Worlds' the 1992 event was rescued by Norman Jenkins when the original Buenos Aires venue reported an outbreak of cholera. Mar del Plata, which had actually been Helen Mary's preferred venue on her pre-regatta visit, proved an ideal alternative.

Numbers were down for various reasons but Ecuador and Paraguay participated for the first time and Croatia appeared under that name.

This was the last of Ben Ainslie's three IODA Worlds and at 63kg he could only achieve 37th place. However this was one of the great national teams of IODA history, containing three of the future Olympic medallists - Nick Rogers and Chris Draper were the others - the 'ferrets' reared by the famous Jim Saltonstall.

The British team of 1992 (with a typical Jim joke!)
l to r: Ben Ainslie, Nick Rogers, Owen Ashton, Verity Slater, Jim Saltonstall, Chris Draper and Sue Ainslie

Almost inevitably the event was won by an Argentinian, Ramón Oliden, who scored five bullets and a second. Intriguingly it was at this event that he met Iker Martinez - placed 13th - whom he would later coach to two Olympic medals.

Organisation, both on and off the water, was superb. Racing was switched to the big outer harbour when conditions got too wild, and the team racing was held in the ideal harbour arena; the only problem being to compete with the sea lions for spectator space. Ashore Christmas was in full swing with lots of parties, culminating in a magnificent asado barbecue on the final night.

Norman and Hazel had created one of the most enjoyable championships and Norman was persuaded to accept a vice-presidency of IODA where he played a major role over the next ten years.

1993 CIUDADELA, SPAIN

179 SAILORS FROM 41 COUNTRIES

The return to Europe created yet another new record, helped by the first appearance under their new flags of Russia, Ukraine, Slovakia and Slovenia. Other first timers were Israel and Myanmar.

Ciudadela, on the western tip of Menorca, was better known as a cruising stopover but the local club did major works to host the event, and ashore showed a very different and more attractive side to the Balaerics than painted in the package holiday brochures of the period.

The surprise winner was Mats Hellman (NED). IODA was still using a two-stage format - qualifying and final rounds - and Mats only ranked 28th in the qualifiers. However with one race to go in the finals he could only be beaten by Esteban Rocha (ARG) whom he match-raced into silver.

As noted elsewhere Mats won in a (van Wettum) hull without buoyancy bag covers which raised some eyebrows especially as he was an 'unknown'. Three years later he won gold at the ISAF Youth Worlds, which suggests that it may have been the sailor not the boat that won.

Claudia Tosi (ITA) took advantage of the rule which allowed the 1992 European champion to enter both the Worlds and Europeans. She retained her title at the latter and took the bronze medal at the Worlds, the second best girls' result until then.

Sardinia's Costa Smeralda lived up to its reputation by providing some of the best and most varied conditions ever, with every wind speed from Force 2 to Force 7: 29 knots were recorded for the opening race.

For the first time the Regatta Committee introduced a single fleet series with 15 races and two discards rather than the conventional but unpopular qualifying races/gold and silver format. With skilled race officering it proved possible to have three consecutive starts of 60 or 61 sailors at each, rather than the 90+ starters which ever increasing entries has created under the previous system.

For only the second time (see chapter 8 for the politics) New Zealand entered a full team. It represented a change of tack for that country which had traditionally regarded the Optimist as a - mostly wooden - basic trainer. Fifteenth place in the Miami Herald (Nations Cup) suggested that they were a team to watch for the future.

The Argentinian domination of the 1990s peaked with all three individual medallists, led by Martín Jenkins, and the team racing prize. This performance would not be equalled for many years. Among the strong Danish team which finished second in both team racing and the Miami Herald was Jonas Warrer whose father Peter had won the 'Worlds' of 1967 & 8. Jonas was to go on to win gold in the 49er at the 2008 Olympics.

Any nervous tension resulting from the first appearance of the 'IOD95' was relieved by the relaxed atmosphere of the beautiful Åland Islands and its welcoming people. The local measurement team was led by the avuncular Ralph Sjöholm who much simplified sail measurement by designing a template, and was to serve IODA for several years as an IM.

Racing was held in an isolated and lovely tree-lined bay in order to keep out of the way of the vast Baltic ferries with the size and wind-shadow of small skyscrapers. The winds after the first three races were predominantly light. Martín Jenkins was one of few to do well in all conditions and survived a DSQ and 33rd to join the elite group of double world champions. The bronze medal taken by Dario Kliba of Croatia was the first of the many to be won by his country in the next few years - Croatia would be placed on the podium for six of the next eight years, perhaps benefiting from the peace after the bitter fighting.

Martín: How can I win if there's no wind?

1996 LANGEBAAN, SOUTH AFRICA 169 SAILORS FROM 39 COUNTRIES

Organised by long-serving Class enthusiast Hans Thijsse and sponsored by Nesquik this was the first and so far only Worlds to be held in Africa. It was a fitting reward for Hans who had had to struggle for years with the exclusion of his country.

Those expecting hot weather got a shock when the southern winter produced almost Scandinavian conditions but the opening ceremony on the waterfront in Cape Town with its haunting African choral music left no doubt which continent we were on.

Charter boats were supplied by Winner, fortunately now fully equipped to produce IOD95s, when a potential local builder pulled out at short notice.

Competition over the fifteen races led to one of the tightest finishes on record, ending with victory by the hugely popular Lisa Westerhof (NED) by a single point when she came third in the final race. Lisa, only the second girl to win the Worlds, was to go on to win bronze in the 2012 Olympics as well as becoming a qualified transatlantic pilot with KLM. Two other Olympic medallists in the fleet were Zach Railey (USA), silver in the Finn and Nicolas Charbonnier (FRA), bronze in the 470, both in 2008.

1997 CARRICKFERGUS, N. IRELAND 189 SAILORS FROM 41 COUNTRIES

Belfast Lough, where weather conditions had been frankly miserable for the Europeans of 1993, produced beautiful sunshine for the Worlds. With the experience of that regatta behind them, the organisers, including the ebullient John Russell and long-time IODA Executive member Curly Morris, provided a seamless experience. To resolve launching problems the local council had invested in a vast pontoon sitting in the harbour under the historic castle.

Peru won the team racing in 1997, 8 & 9

The event was won by future Melges 24 star Luca Bursic (ITA) but the surprise victory came from Peru in the team-racing. With the advantage of comprising sailors from a single club in Lima they took the team discipline to a new level They would win the next two team racing worlds and establish the norm of Peru versus Argentina for the finals of many years to come.

The outstanding future Olympian was Siren Sundby of Norway in 10th place. She would progress seemingly effortlessly through gold at the ISAF Youth World Championship to Olympic gold in the Europe Class at the age of 22.

The return to the ever popular venue of Portugal saw a new record, 44 countries. The event was again heavily sponsored by Nesquik and organised at a previously unused venue by the Associação Naval Lisboa with a lot of help from long-serving Class secretary and IODA vice-president Mimi Santos.

For the first time China sent a full team. It was recorded that lack of experience led to them incurring several RRS42 disqualifications but the performance of Shen Xiaoying earned her girls' bronze. She was to go on to be the first Chinese representative in the Olympic single-hander in 2004. Bermuda returned after the absence of many years, following the foundation of a Bermuda Optimist Dinghy Association led by the Kirkland family.

The convincing winner was Mattia Pressich, at 34kg the lightest known champion ever.

The first Worlds to be held in the Caribbean offered IODA the chance to promote Optimist sailing in the region. The 1990s had already seen considerable progress. In 1993 St. Thomas Y.C. in the U.S. Virgin Islands had established a Caribbean regatta with participants from Barbados, Guadeloupe, Puerto Rico and St. Maarten, with in the following year Antigua, Puerto Rico and the British Virgin Islands.

But none of these had yet attended the Worlds or even the North Americans. So IODA decided to offer free entry and charter at this Worlds to two sailors from each of the Caribbean countries. The offer was accepted by Barbados, Cuba, Guatemala, Puerto Rico, St. Lucia, Trinidad and the USVI. Unsurprisingly none of them did very well but the long term effect was to be beyond expectations.

Low cost airfares from Paris and mandatory charter of Winners made the venue highly accessible from Europe, and previous records for attendance were smashed. Sailing, under the watchful eye of Michel Barbier, was *magnifique*. Mattia Pressich, who had gained 6kg and 17cm during the year, retained his title easily by a margin of 27 points over Tonci Stipanovic who was to place 4th in the 2012 Olympic Laser event. There were at least 14 future Olympians in the fleet but few noticed future gold medallist 12-year old Lijia Xu back in 154th place.

Participation

Participation at the Worlds rose from an average of 27 countries in the 1980s to 40 in the 1990s. This was due partly to the newly independent members from Europe (shown in italics below) but also to more regular participation from the fleets developed earlier. This in turn may have resulted from the general reduction in airfares combined with the increasingly satisfactory provision of charter boats.

Known first time participants were:

1991: Algeria, Cyprus, New Zealand	1995: *Belarus*, Hong Kong, *Lithuania*, India
1992: Ecuador, Paraguay	1996: Myanmar, Kuwait
1993: Russia, *Slovakia*, *Slovenia*, *Ukraine*	1998: *Latvia*

and in 1999 as a result of developments described above:

Barbados, Guatemala, Puerto Rico, St. Lucia, Trinidad, U.S.V.I.

Continental Championships

The major growth in the three existing continental championships took place in the late 1980s in Europe and the early 1990s in the Americas. By 1990 in Europe and 1995 in the Americas, participation had reached almost 100% of the then existing member countries.

Europeans

The rapid growth in the 1980s, from less than 80 participants in 1983 to 218 in 1990, meant that almost all European countries were by then sending full teams, so increases in the 1990s were more modest.

	1990	1992	1999	
'West' European	145	140	168	
'East' European*	45	36	42	* Former Comecon & Yugoslavia
Non-European	28	44	22**	** abnormally low, probably due to the
	218	220	232	Worlds being in Martinique
(Girls)	(74)	(80)	(85)	

Until around 1993 this European Championship was in practice organised by a European grouping and the event sought little input from the IODA Regatta Committee. However from 1988 non-European teams were admitted, and rising expectations of the quality of racing led to it being brought fully under IODA control. The all-important choice of venue was now made at the IODA AGM by the official representatives of the European countries. There were some memorable regattas with a wide range of countries leading:

	Venue		*Boys*		*Girls*	
1990	Flensburg	GER	Jurica Tunjic*	YUG	Signe Groth*	DEN
1991	Anzio	ITA	**Gabrio Zandoná**	ITA	Emma Aspington*	SWE
1992	Svendborg	DEN	Alex v.d.Camme	NED	Karoline Rydell*	SWE
1993	Belfast L.	GBR	Tomas Gunst	BEL	Claudia Tosi*	ITA
1994	Silivri	TUR	Jess Anderson*	DEN	***Lobke Berkhout****	NED
1995	Andijk	NED	Maxim Pidgurskiy*	UKR	Liat Ribman	ISR
1996	Palma	ESP	David Kearley	ESP	***Siren Sundby****	NOR
1997	Piran	SLO	Jaume Tous Gonzalez	ESP	***Siren Sundby****	NOR
1998	Split	CRO	**Ivan K-Gaspic***	CRO	***Evi van Acker***	BEL
1999	Mati	GRE	Nick Thompson	GBR	***Giulia Conti****	ITA

* = open champion. The winners shown are the top Europeans. The outright winners were often Argentinian boys (1993, 1996, 1997 & 1999) or Brasilian girls (1995, 1998) in a decade when South Americans also dominated the Worlds.

It is notable that, despite these sailors being on the *second* teams of their countries, several champions, especially girls' champions but including Bambi (I. K-Gaspic), were future Olympians.

These are shown in **bold**, with those in ***bold italics*** future Olympic medallists.

Bambi

As noted in chapter 4 the championship created in 1973 had expanded in the mid-1980s to include Chile (hosts in 1985) and Peru (hosts in 1989). Venezuela participated intermittently and by 1989 Ecuador also attended. Visitors from the USA had taken part throughout, with Mark Mendelblatt gaining the open title in 1987 & 8.

In 1990 Salinas, Ecuador proved a popular venue and the event attracted entries from Mexico and South Africa (still sadly excluded from the Worlds) as well as Colombia to increase the fleet to 96 sailors. But not all South American countries attended regularly and it was not until 1994 that all nine, including Paraguay, participated in the same year.

	1989	1990	1995	1999
S. Americans	} 54	77	106	114
N. Americans			26	31
Non-American	0	} 19	2	15
	54	96	134	160

This was a period of South American, especially Argentinian, ascendancy in the Optimist world and the only gold medallists from North America were girls, Christina Bickley in 1993 and Amanda Clark in 1995.

	Venue		*Over-all*		*Girls*	
1990	Salinas	ECU	Diego Dumais	ARG	Veronica Olivella	URU
1991	Porto Alegre	BRA	Agustin Krevisky	ARG	Maria Fernanda	ARG
1992	Montevideo	URU	Juan D. Figueroa	ARG	Martha Martins R.	ARG
1993	Mar del Plata	ARG	Miguel Cadeiras	ARG	Paula Mariño	URU
1994	Lima	PER	Federico Perez	ARG	Christina Damiani	PER
1995	Algarrobo	CHI	Lucas Gomez	ARG	Mariana Tieri	ARG
1996	Salinas	ECU	Alejandro Sole	ARG	Roberta Borges	BRA
1997	P. del Este	URU	Matías Buhler	ARG	Claudia Rafaniello	URU
1998	Cartagena	COL	Sebastian Rezzano	ARG	Roberta Borges	BRA
1999	Buenos Aires	ARG	Fernando Gwodz	ARG	Roberta Borges	BRA

From the above it came as no surprise when Roberta Borges became in 1999 the first ever non-European to win girls' gold at the Optimist Worlds.

Cartagena 1998

North Americans

With the expansion of Optimists in the USA beyond their traditional bases, the fleet created in Mexico in 1987 and the renaissance of Bermuda, the North Americans became more truly continental. Carlos Prieto and future Olympian Tania Elias Calles became in 1994 the first Mexicans to win the continental titles. Two years later Stu Colie from New Jersey and Mary Ridenour from Pennsylvania seem to have been the first non-Floridan U.S. winners. Numbers of participants are less meaningful for this championship than others, as much depended on the venue; for example southern teams seem to have been reluctant to travel to Vancouver. Also entry limits varied, for example in 1995 no less than 145 USA sailors participated.

	Venue		Over-all		Girls	
1990	Toronto?	CAN	Fred Bickley*	USA	Mallory Mestayer*	USA
1991	Cancún	MEX	Alan Uram*	USA	Anne Marie Casesa*	USA
1992	Shelter I., NY	USA	David Ames	USA	Heather Boynton*	USA
1993	Kingston	CAN	Christina Bickley*	USA	Christina Bickley*	USA
1994	V, de Bravo	MEX	Carlos Prieto	MEX	**Tania Elias Calles***	MEX
1995	Little Egg NJ	USA	*Zach Railey**	USA	**Amanda Clark**	USA
1996	Vancouver	CAN	Stu Colie*	USA	Mary Ridenour*	USA
1997	Acapulco	MEX	Diego Prieto*	MEX	Isabelle Garand	CAN
1998	Hamilton	BER	**Erik Storck***	USA	Kitty Lovelace*	USA
1999	C. Christi, TX	USA	**Trevor Moore**	USA	Elizabeth Kempton	USA

* Also open North American champion.

Perhaps the most remarkable of the above results was Zach Railey in 1995. The future Olympic medallist won the championship at the age of just 11 years.

Asians

The IODA Asian Championship was created by Ng Ser Miang in 1990. It built on the success of the ASEAN (Association of S.E. Asian Nations) championship developed by Al Chandler four years earlier and on the 1989 Worlds in Japan. The first edition was an immediate success with teams from nine Asian nations, every IODA member at that time. Teams, except for the host nation, were limited to five sailors. The winner, Tan Wearn Haw, is the current CEO of Singapore Sailing.

Other countries joined in as follows:

1992:	Korea and Myanmar	1994	Pakistan
1993	Chinese Taipei	1996	Kyrgyzstan

	Venue		Over-all		Girls	
1990	Singapore	SIN	**Tan Wearn Haw**	SIN	Ng Xua Hui	SIN
1991	Qingdao	CHN	Ryan Tan	MAS	Ng Xuan Hui	SIN
1992	Pattaya	THA	Umiko Arakawa	JPN	Ng Xuan Hui	SIN
1993	Hiroshima	JPN	**Tetsuya Matsunaga**	JPN	Yuki Sanbu	JPN
1994	Kinabalu	MAS	Ryan Tan	MAS	Yuki Sanbu	JPN
1995	P. Dickson	MAS	Ryan Tan	MAS	Ayako Kamiya	JPN
1996	Karachi	PKN	Jiang Linhua	CHN	**Shen Xiaoying**	CHN
1997	Busan	KOR	Shiori Kondou	JPN	Shiori Kondou	JPN
1998	Shanghai	CHN	**Shen Xiaoying**	CHN	**Shen Xiaoying**	CHN
1999	Karachi	PKN	Andrew Yeow	MAS	*Xu Lijia*	CHN

Already there were hopes of westward expansion into the Gulf but this would have to await the new decade.

Team Pakistan

Photo: Team Pakistan in 1999. Teamleader Capt. Abdur Rehman Arshad, future vice-president of IODA.

Other Regattas

The Nordic Championship, probably the oldest regional event, continued to promote regional sailing but a Mediterranean, established in 1987, was finally discontinued due to lack of support from France and Spain. The way forward proved in general to be regattas open to all. The ongoing reduction in airfares, the increasing availability of top-quality charter boats, and better communication - initially by fax, later by internet - led to the growth of ever-larger 'unofficial' regattas. In particular off-season events at (hopefully) warmer venues increasingly made sailing an all-year sport.

Among the earliest were the Christmas regattas at San Remo, Italy (1986) and the Orange Bowl in Miami, while at Easter the Meeting in Riva del Garda, founded in 1982 and already with around 400 participants in 1989 and Braassemermeer in Holland, dating from 1985 and with 315 sailors by 1990, were already showing the way. In 1992 IODA started to publish a list of major regattas and listed 18 events (other than national championships) attended by five or more countries. By 1999 there were nearly fifty such events . . . and internet communication was still in its infancy.

As the *Optiworld* newsletter repeatedly reminded readers: "Who needs to get selected?" Just as a holiday an Optimist regatta (with a little obligatory culture on the side) is likely to be more fun than trailing around after the parents. Exchange trips too are likely to be more rewarding if there is a shared interest. As one parent wrote of a visit from a rather earnest young world champion: "I think we helped him chill out a bit".

Chapter 6: the 'IOD95' Project

In order to understand how and why IODA developed in the 1990s its unique and effective system of ensuring a strict one-design it is necessary to go into some detail.

The background

In March 1992 Helen Mary appeared before the IYRU Executive and was told that the cost of competitive Optimists needed to be reduced.

That October the Technical Officers of the IYRU reported that *"there was still great concern over the plans to reduce the price of competitive boats. Members reiterated that there should be a licensed builder system for GRP boats and the manufacturing process should be simplified, both to ensure that the agreed objectives would be achieved."*

The key word was "competitive". Class-legal Optimists were available in every major market at very low prices. But in recent years many people had come to believe that "competitive" meant Winner (or possibly Lange) and a *top-of-the-range* Winner was expensive, especially in many countries if bought through a distributor.

However the IYRU Centreboard Boat Committee (CBC) had in the same year discussed the general subject of licensed builders and revealingly minuted that:

"It was agreed that for licensing systems to work properly, the IYRU must be able and prepared to take action against builders (i.e. terminate licences) which fail to abide by their contracts to build in accordance with the specifications and rules"

"It was also suggested that periodical inspections on the builder's premises should be made to check that the builders are building in accordance with the specification and class rules." and

"It was further noted that considerable funding would be required if the IYRU were to undertake to inspect all its licensed builders on a regular basis and that the class association is best equipped to supervise construction practices within the licensee's works."

In plain terms this suggested that the IYRU continued to advocate a licensed builder system (which had been rejected by Viggo back in 1973) but knew it lacked the resources and perhaps even the will to administer it.

The CBC knew that the problem went deeper and identified a major part of any problems with Classes with multiple builders. It minuted:

"[in a] one-design *Class the builder's interest is fundamentally in exploiting class rules to produce a superior product with which to compete"* and that some Olympic Classes *"are essentially one 'major builder' classes in which relatively wide tolerances have been explored and optimized."*

It was clear that there was some incompatibility between the belief that the solution to any Optimist problem was a licensed builder system and the admission that lack of control by the IYRU had led to two of its Olympic Classes becoming *"essentially one 'major builder' classes"*, with the sort of pricing which could result from a virtual monopoly.

If the price of competitive Optimists was to be reduced, more thought was needed and IODA conducted extensive research into prices. What it found was that:

- the Optimist Class had had, for most of the 1980s 'one major builder', Winner Optimists, whose product was used by up to 80% of sailors seeking to qualify for the Worlds.
- Customers in most countries had to buy from a distributor. If that distributor had a monopoly, either as a sole agent or because they were the only one to import in bulk, they could charge what

they liked.

- Winner themselves had a variety of models. The most expensive was nearly 80% dearer than the basic model. Part of the difference was due to better spars, sails and perhaps foils. But their most expensive *hull* was over 40% more than the basic hull and there was little evidence that it was any faster: charter boats at regattas were usually the basic hull and often achieved excellent results.

In fact, unknown to the IYRU and perhaps even to IODA, the Optimist was that year gradually beginning to move away from the 'one major builder' situation. Firstly from 1988 Lange Argentina had developed a competitive boat to service the rapidly growing South American market and was beginning to penetrate the North American and European markets. Then between 1992 and 1995 several other builders, notably Finessa Sweden, Nautivela Italy, Naaix Spain and van Wettum Holland, captured at least a share of their large national markets and achieved some success in exporting. However, as is usual in marketing, these new competitors (or their distributors) tended to fix their price at just below that of the market leader. Winner continued to dominate many markets, not least the British homeland of the IYRU where they supplied over 65% of *all* hulls registered in 1990/1.

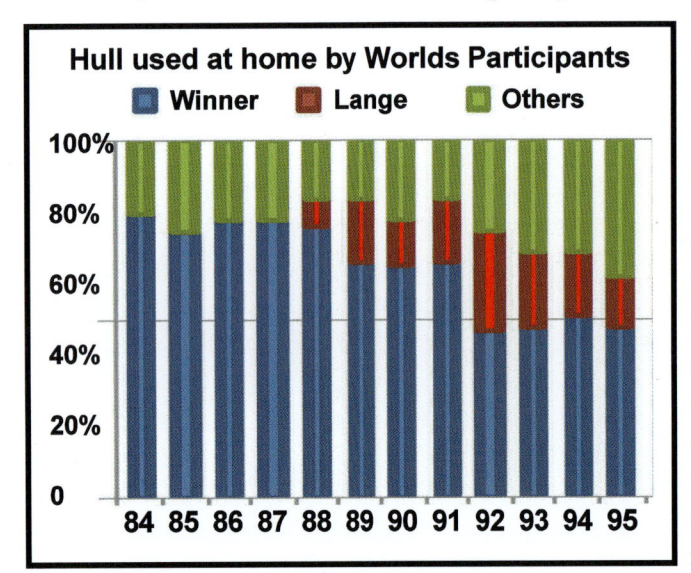

What was needed to reduce the "cost of competitive Optimists" was more competition between builders, a very strict one-design with as many builders as possible around the world producing an identical boat. John Teeling, then professor of international marketing at Dublin University (and later to make a fortune from breaking a near-monopoly in the production of Irish whiskey) compared the situation to Aspirin. Everybody could produce the basic product at low cost; what increased the price was branding of supposedly superior variations - New! Improved! Aspirin Plus!

Technical Specification

IODA was fortunate in having the technical expertise to analyse the elements needed for a strict one-design. The chair of the technical committee was Patrick Bergmans, a professor of engineering at Ghent University, and he could rely on the creative thinking of Fred Kats, who had already simplified and improved the way an Optimist was rigged. Both were parents of successful ex-Optimist and Olympic sailors.

Fred & Dominique

Their fundamental thinking on one design was:
- to maintain the successful exterior dimensions of the leading builders
- to create a boat which was as far as possible entirely moulded. Moulding led to the possibility of very tight tolerances
- to expose the two areas where measurement had previously been difficult, the buoyancy bag covers

and the centreboard case
- to eliminate wood from the GRP hull: wood, as Fred commented, is an exotic material
- to be able to measure laminates, and
- most importantly, to ensure that the revised design was exactly the same speed as the existing competitive Optimists. It would have been a disaster if the thousands of older boats became uncompetitive.

There was much consultation with builders at the Europeans in the summer of 1992 and outline proposals were agreed by the AGM in Argentina. Fred Kats worked with the Dutch builder Jan van Wettum, and a crucial vindication of the possibility of removing the buoyancy covers came when Mats Hellman (NED) sailed a van Wettum without such covers to victory in the 1993 Worlds. Two experimental hulls of the proposed design were built free of charge by van Wettum and quietly sailed at French regattas by 'middle of the fleet' sailors under the supervision of Dominique Langlois, now chairman of the IODA Technical Committee, and their performance carefully studied.

Mats - no buoyancy covers!

The development process was not without some crises. At one stage it was found that the new plans had been 'frozen' by the CAD program used and a critical weekend was spent while the data was re-entered in the studio of a leading yacht designer.

In November 1994 Curly Morris, now chair of the IODA Technical Committee, presented the new plans and rules to the IYRU and they were approved with the timetable that building to the new specification was *permitted* from 1 March 1995 and *mandatory* from 1 March 1996.

Introduction

The critical test of the new 'IOD95' was the Worlds in Mariehamn, Finland in the summer of 1995. Only two builders, Vene Björndahl of Finland and Keith Elliott from New Zealand (who produced the spectacular 'All Black' hull shown) had had the courage to build the new boat. Björndahl was the official charter boat but the Argentinian team had Langes (made under licence by the renowned Snipe builder Persson in Denmark) and the Brasilians had Winners. However many countries, including Spain and Uruguay, accepted Björndahls. The results of the championship brought huge relief to the Technical Committee. The top 20 figured five Winners, two Langes . . . and five Björndahls. All the signs were that the new design had indeed the same potential speed as the best existing boats.

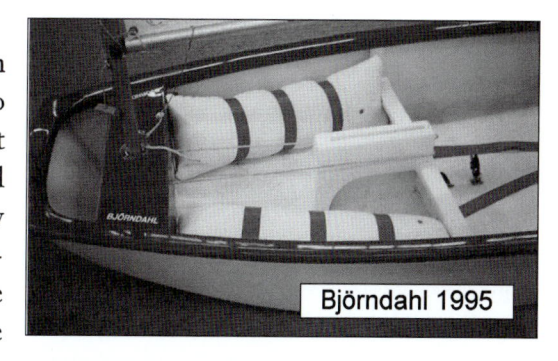

Björndahl 1995

Winner accepted the reality and in November had prototypes from two moulds approved. The rush was on. In the first six months of 1996 ten builders got approval including, critically, McLaughlin and Vanguard in the USA. By the end of the year yet another eight had done so, including Lange (now re-named Rio Tecna). The Optimist world had 20 builders in 15 countries on four continents.

As the CBC had identified, control and inspection were the key to one-design. After the first few prototypes had been measured in Holland, IODA reached the conclusion that this inspection must take place in the builder's works. This did indeed, as the CBC had noted, require "considerable funding". Fortunately IODA had just acquired the Nesquik sponsorship and could divert its existing training budget to the inspection programme. It was thus able to offer to any builder free prototype inspection at its works for their first prototype.

To undertake this extensive travel schedule, IODA hired David Harte who, unlike many measurers, was a fully qualified and experienced boatbuilder. In his first year he spent no less than 86 days abroad, not just inspecting prototypes but using his expertise to advise on correcting faults and ensuring ongoing consistency. Each builder had to supply elaborate cut-out samples *before* David's visit to show the laminates and moulding-joins, and it proved possible by examining these over many long evenings in the Wilkes's kitchen to avoid premature inspection. To train national measurers for ongoing inspection a big seminar attended by measurers from 18 countries was held near Amsterdam, but perhaps more importantly David also undertook detailed measurer training during his visits.

Administration

Measuring prototypes needed to be supplemented by ongoing measurement of production boats. This had to fit within the IYRU structure of national measurers authorised by the National Sailing Association (MNA) which then issued measurement certificates. IODA supplemented this by creating a Registration Book which included the actual measurement form, i.e. the precise dimensions of the individual boat as measured by the national measurer. This Registration Book was unique to the numbers on the ISAF plaque and the moulds used, the numbers of which were moulded into the hull. IODA required that this Book be produced at all its regattas and at these regattas the IODA team of IYRU-qualified International Measurers re-measured in full at least one sample boat from each manufacturer and compared their findings with the measurement form in the Registration Book.

Significant variations were rare but when they occurred they were referred to the MNA who had authorised the original measurer. Reactions varied. In one case the MNA disqualified the measurer and even suspended him from membership of the federation. In a second case the MNA accepted that a measurer from a neighbouring MNA had to be used. However one MNA insisted on supporting its measurer despite clear evidence of, at best, negligence. The reaction of IODA was simply to cease supply of Registration Books and IYRU plaques to until and unless a solution was found. IODA was, to quote again the CBC, "*able and prepared to take action against builders . . . which fail to abide by their contracts to build in accordance with the specifications and rules*".

The impact

The objective was to phase in the new one-design, and existing hulls remained competitive. Only as they reached their normal retirement date were they replaced by 'IOD95s'. However by 1998, while Winner and Lange retained - and would continue to retain - significant market share, a majority of sailors trialing for their national teams used boats bought elsewhere, usually directly from a more local builder.

Indeed already actual results soon confirmed the equality of different builders and that the market believed in it. By the Europeans of 1997, for example, the top 20 sailors (top 10 boys and girls) between them sailed ten different makes of boat.

The Optimist was no longer in any danger of being a 'one major builder' Class.

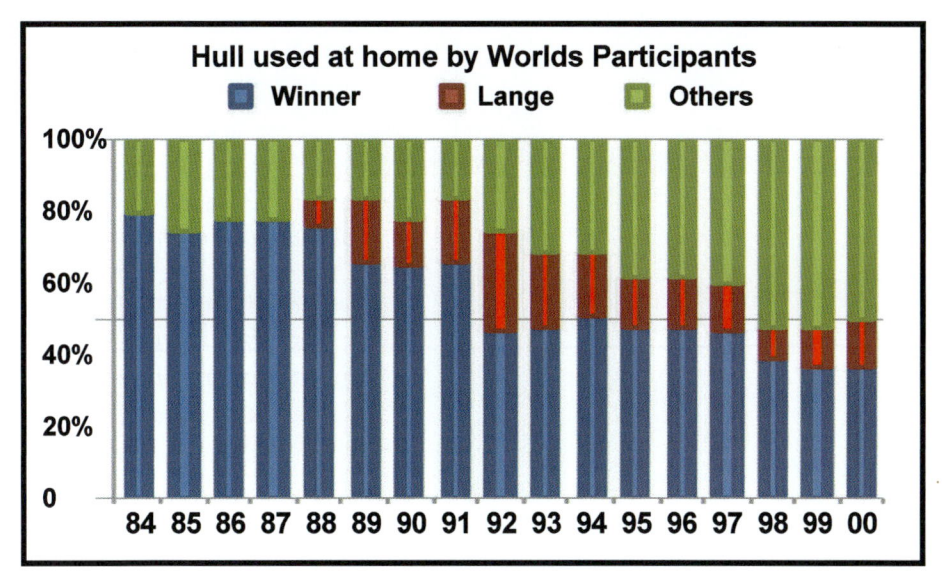

Charter

The acceptance that all boats were equal had a radical effect on the cost of participation at IODA World and European championships (charter was usually mandatory elsewhere). While the option of charter had long been available and the quality of charter boats had steadily improved, sailors were reluctant to charter and felt obliged to bring their own boats as long as they believed that the charter boats might be inferior. Now they could be sure that those boats, whoever the supplier, would be as good as any others and the decision to charter or not became a question of relative cost.

Some builders continued to try to prove that their products were faster by offering lower or zero charter prices to the most promising sailors but IODA quickly prevented this practice by insisting that sailors must use either their own boats, properly registered in their own country, or the official charter boats supplied by the organisers.

Organisers too now had a choice of charter boat suppliers and could even split the charter boat order and allocate boats at random. For example at the 2006 North Americans in Puerto Rico the (mandatory) charter boats were 50% McLaughlins and 50% Rio Tecnas: the average placing of sailors

Bringing your own boats was no longer necessary

At the 2007 Europeans in Greece, eight countries from north and west Europe opted to charter rather than haul their own boats. Eight of the top 20 sailors used charter boats.

using each was just four places different (93rd versus 97th). A similar equality was found between the charter boats supplied by Nautivela and Cantiere Nordest at the 2007 Worlds in Sardinia.

Prices

For a brief period prices actually rose. Prices were, as IODA had identified, largely dictated by distributors not the builders themselves, so it took a while for such distributors to realise that an exclusive agency was no longer a licence to print money. By 1997 there were builders producing identical boats in most major markets except Germany and Japan, so many sailors could buy directly from a manufacturer in their own or a nearby country.

In 1998 the IYRU published an article by IODA claiming that prices had fallen by around 25%. No one disputed that claim.

Trade Mark

Following the success of the 'IOD95' project IODA needed more than ever to distinguish Optimists from the wide variety of other boats being sold misusing the Optimist name. The only existing protection of the name was the design copyright assigned to the IYRU back in 1973 under a contract which specified that the IYRU would take legal action to protect it *at IODA's expense*. This would have been prohibitively expensive, and in any case the copyright of a design which had been gradually developed was of doubtful value even under English law.

A meeting with Paolo Sangiorgi, an Optimist father (his son was to win the 2000 Europeans) and a director of the San Pellegrino water company, suggested an alternative. In 1994 the European Union had established the snappily named 'Office for Harmonisation in the Internal Market' (OHIM) which could register a *trade mark* valid throughout the Union and, through the Madrid Protocol, most other countries in the world. Moreover Paolo put IODA in touch with the Italian patent agents, Societá Italiana Brevetti, who would act for IODA at very low cost (Thanks, Paolo!). An application, approved by the IYRU, was made in 1998 for the trademark name 'Optimist' covering not only boats and sails but also events. After some delay when the Spanish tobacco brand Fortuna claimed prior rights (incredibly by today's standards it had once sponsored Optimist sailing in Spain), the IODA trademark was finally registered in 2000. In the new decade this trade mark protection was to prove very valuable, not least because it was valid under Chinese law.

Chapter 7: the World Championship Debate

For twelve years from 1992 the IODA World Championship attracted sustained attention from, reputedly, the IYRU/ISAF Executive. The relevant minutes were as follows:

1992-1994

IYRU Executive October 1992:

"Members were concerned to see children competing in world championships and asked the Youth Committee to consider the matter."

IYRU Youth Sailing Committee November 1994:

"IMPACT OF TOP LEVEL SAILING

The impact of top level sailing on young people was considered and the International Optimist Class Association was invited to present their paper on the subject.

It was felt that the policy of IODA in managing International Regattas including Worlds, Continental and Regionals is very much supported and it is a means by which they can ensure that the pressures which are imposed on young people can be kept under control and within limits which are acceptable. Furthermore, if IODA did not do what they are doing within a highly respected and organised structure, then some other less well intentioned organisation may take over.

Decision

The Optimist programme as presently practised was supported by the Committee and it was considered that participation in the IODA Championships had no adverse affects in the large majority of children in these age groups."

1997

ISAF Executive June 1997:

"The President expressed that the ISAF should endeavour to provide a direction for sailors in the 13-17 year old age group, who invariably have no clear indication what boats to sail in and how to progress to after the Optimist. The possibility of developing an ISAF Junior Championship was raised."

Quite how this was compatible with its 1992 concern about "children competing in world championships", given that IODA had shown that over 90% of participants at its Worlds were 13-15, was never explained. The Youth Committee expressed polite interest but approved a submission from the Deutscher Segler Verband which rejected the idea.

2001-4

ISAF Executive November 2001:

"8 (c) International Optimist Class

The Executive Committee considered the upper [sic] *age limit for Optimist class events. Members of the Executive Committee expressed some concern on whether this age group should participate in world championships.*

Decision: The Executive Committee request that the Youth Sailing Training & Development Committee investigate a revised upper [sic] *age limit for the Optimist class events."*

ISAF Executive August-November 2002

"Age Limit and World Championship Events

The Executive Committee re-considered the age limit at world championship level events. Some Member

National Authorities (MNAs) have expressed concern that, for instance, the Optimist Class has become too autonomous to the detriment of the individual sailors. To compete at the highest level is extremely expensive and the broad base and/or entry-level sailor has difficulties in maintaining their status in the class. There is some suggestion that there is an optimum weight for sailing in the Optimist class, and some sailors therefore control their weight with the use of strict diet and/or drugs. The Executive Committee agree that this pressure is detrimental both to the image of the sport and to the promotion of the sport at junior/entry level.

The Executive Committee prepared submission 063-02P on age limits at world championships.

SUBMISSION 063-02P

Age Limit and World Championship Events

There is a minimum age limit of 15 years for all sailors competing in world championship events. Competitors shall be over the age limit on 1 January of the year in which the event is held.

REASON: "It is the opinion of the Executive Committee that the increased pressure on young people to compete at top-level events has an adverse impact on sailing at entry and junior level."

The submission was rejected outright by the Events Committee. The recommendation of the Youth Committee was to limit participation to those over 12 at the end of the year. The Executive withdrew the proposal but it was agreed that it would appoint a Working Party to consider the subject. Two years later in 2004 the Working Party reported that it:

"has concluded High Level Sport places demands on Youth Sailors and their supporters, but that these demands are not disproportionate and are, indeed, less than in many other sports."

While the proposal 063-02 had been formally withdrawn, a proposal (062-02) which included the ban on under-12s was still on the table. It was rejected by Council by 31 votes to 5 with 2 abstentions.

The background

It may seem strange that proposals to ban the IODA World Championship were repeatedly rejected by every committee which considered them (with the possible exception of an Under-12 ban at the Youth Committee). The final vote of 31 votes to 5 with 2 abstentions means that not even the 7-person Executive was fully in support of proposals which were claimed to originate from it.

The motivation behind the proposals is suggested by views expressed on the online magazine *Scuttlebutt*. In October 2002 Paul Henderson, vice-president in 1992 and president from 1994, wrote:

"The Age Limit proposal is to address the problem of the Olympic Classes, ISAF Events and those classes [he specifically mentioned the Optimist] *that endeavour to dominate a whole sector of the sailing world." "The corollary of that is that when a class becomes Olympic or demands to be the class that the MNAs designate for an age group or an ISAF Event they become partners of ISAF and the MNAs and lose a portion of their autonomy and an age limit must be considered."*

The age limit proposal had in fact nothing to do with the Olympic Classes and only marginally to do with other ISAF Events. The Optimist Class had never demanded "to be the class that the MNAs designate for an age group or an ISAF Event". Many MNAs had so designated the Optimist but that was their choice.

In 2004, again on Scuttlebutt (no. 1662), Arturo Delgado (ESP), a vice-president in 1992 and still a Council member in 2004, wrote:

"Because of the big influence the Optimist Class has on kids and future great sailors, I've maintained for years that ISAF, Continental Federations and MNAs must have more control on the development and activities of the Class."

But the ISAF Council, the body "responsible for managing the sport of Yachting", at no time showed any significant support for these views. Indeed it is interesting that the 2002 AGM of US Sailing formally resolved:

> *"US Sailing is opposed to ISAF rules or regulations that disenfranchise class organizations and their members. ISAF classes should retain their autonomy and class management."*, and:
>
> *"US Sailing opposes any move by ISAF to place additional age limits on participation in World Championship events."*

Continental Championships

It is also possible that certain individuals within the IYRU/ISAF even sought to "disenfranchise" International Classes from running continental events. Certainly in May 1998 it was minuted that:

> *"Council approve the placement of the <u>restoration</u>* [underlining by author] *of the rights of classes to hold continental championships . . . as follows:*
>
> *7.? International and Recognised Class Associations have the sole right to hold continental championships of their class, these being class events as defined in (new) Regulation 10.5.6."*

Chapter 8: 2000-2007

Administration 2000-2007

Helen Mary retired from the presidency in 1998 - presidents and vice-presidents are limited to a 10-year term - and also retired from the position of vice-chair of the ISAF Classes Committee to which she had been elected in 1994 (incidentally the first woman ever to be *elected* to any position in the ISAF). However she still attended ISAF conferences in her new role of president of the Women's International Match Racing Association, working to promote WMR for inclusion in the Olympics. In view of IODA's negotiations with the ISAF Executive she continued also to represent the Optimist Class at ISAF meetings and critically she was a member of the Working Party on Submission 063-02 described above. She was in fact to return to Classes work in 2008 when she was again elected vice-chair of the ISAF Classes Committee.

Michel & René

New president René Kluin had worked with IODA since 1986 and had already been a member of the Executive for seven years. The transition for his first term of office was seamless with Michel Barbier stepping into the vacant role of chair of the Regatta Committee. Helen Mary accompanied Robert to all meetings and remained an ex-officio non-voting member of the Executive, but the need to support her with regatta organisation was met by the election to the Regatta Committee in 1999 of Nazli Imre, president of the Turkish Sailing Federation and future ISAF vice-president.

In 1999 the Executive was slightly re-structured so that each of the vice-presidents was now to be from a different continent, i.e. Europe, the Americas and Africa/Asia/Oceania.

Despite some changes - the temporary replacement of Mimi Santos, unseated at the fractious Worlds of 2001 but reinstated two years later, the retirement under the 10-year rule of Norman Jenkins, replaced by future IODA president Peter Barclay from Peru, and the election of David Booth (RSA) as a vice-president - IODA saw few administrative changes in the early part of the period. Michel and Curly remained highly influential whether or not they were formally members of the Executive.

IODA's ability to fund its builder inspection programme was further improved when the 2003 AGM decided unanimously to cease paying any share of the ISAF plaque fee to the country of the builder. The control of boat building, local in the days of the wooden Optimist, was now undertaken

AGM 2002: l to r: René, Robert, Hans, Peter and Michel, with Italian Class secretary Norberto Foletti

almost entirely by IODA itself.

In 2005 the Executive conducted a 'Brainstorming Session' with the help of future ISAF vice-president Chris Atkins to identify SWOT. One of the weaknesses identified was the need to plan succession of key personnel, especially given the intention of Robert to retire in 2006 and the consequent additional loss of Helen Mary's expertise.

The discussion anticipated a problem which arose almost immediately. In the spring of 2006 René fell seriously ill. While he was sorely missed, the Wilkes had not yet retired and were able to keep the show running until the AGM at the year-end in Montevideo could elect Peter Barclay as the new president. Under the circumstances Robert agreed to continue as secretary until 2008.

In the spring of 2008 he retired (except for development and some trade mark work) and a new secretary was selected in the person of Sally Burnett, a senior ISAF race official and committee member.

Progress 2000-2007

The final years of this chronicle started with a celebration of the millennium which, together with the 'Caribbean Worlds' of 1999, led to much progress in Africa and the Caribbean. There were also positive developments in Oceania, including but not confined to New Zealand and Australia, in the Arabian Gulf and in Eastern Europe.

IODA championships were notable for the much wider range of nationalities achieving good results. The increasing number of nations seeking to participate required some re-structuring and in general the quality of events was improved. The results achieved by the top girls showed a remarkable improvement and quotas for female participation were extended.

On the technical side the long-sought standardisation of foils was finally achieved. Action was taken to control some undesirable innovations in sailmaking, and the one-design hull was carefully policed. Production of Optimists increased and the benefits of the 'free construction' policy were seen in the reduction in ex-factory prices as a result of more boat building in Asia, both for export and local growth.

Development in newer markets was helped by the introduction of IODA subsidies under the '6 for 5' programme.

The millennium Worlds

"Robert's Mad Idea" was the title he gave to a proposal he made in late 1998 to celebrate the forthcoming millennium. It proposed to offer free entry, accommodation and charter for the 2000 Worlds for two sailors from any country which had never before entered. The record attendance in 1998 for the event was 44 countries: how many more could they attract?

The answer, after it had been decided to extend the offer to countries which had participated only once before, sometimes in the distant past but also including the Caribbean countries helped in 1999, was nineteen:

Algeria	British V.I.	Belarus	India
Egypt	Barbados	Cyprus	Pakistan
Morocco	Guatemala	Latvia	U.A.Emirates
Tunisia	Puerto Rico	Lithuania	
	Trinidad	Malta	
	U.S. Virgin I.	Moldova	

The total attendance was 59 countries. This set a new record for any single-Class regatta.

As a long term promotion of the Class the project was an success. All of the above countries except Moldova participated at later IODA events and, as shown below, the experience had significant effects on later development.

But IODA learned a lesson. Mixing relative novices with the highly trained top teams was neither enjoyable for the sailors nor easy for the race officers. Henceforward IODA decided to concentrate on developing continental and regional championships and to direct less-experienced countries towards them. Entry to the Worlds could not exclude sailors from any country, but future IODA grants would be only for these more local events. Younger sailors should not be automatically excluded - there were too many examples of genuinely talented 11-year olds - but in future sailors under 12 had to show that they had gained national selection on merit.

Worlds 2003

IODA had learned some lessons: but the experiment had valuable lasting results.

Expansion in the new century

The stimulus of the Millenium Project and the 1999 Caribbean Worlds had immediate effects. There was also interesting progress elsewhere.

Africa

The presence in 2000 of four 'new' African teams, together with those from South Africa and Zimbabwe, coincided with the election of David Booth from South Africa as a vice-president. Discussions were held which resulted in an invitation from Abdelhamid Morsi of Egypt to host a new IODA African Championship in Alexandria the following year. All six countries duly sent teams, with the addition of the Seychelles to give 40 African sailors. IODA provided expert support, sending Nuno Reis IM and Ewen Stamp from the Regatta Committee as well as David to help with organisation.

The potential for growth was evident. Great support was given by Mohamed Azzoug, the very popular Algerian IJ who was to become the first president of the African Sailing Confederation. IODA continued to give free entry and charter to each country when it first participated and to send race officials and IODA representatives. In 2003 Kenya and Uganda were added to the participants, in 2005 Tanzania and Mauritius, and in 2008 Angola, Senegal and the French territory of Réunion.

Results were perhaps rather unexpected:

	Venue		Over-all		Girls	
2001	Alexandria	EGY	Lalaoui Abdallah	ALG	Carla Dyer	RSA
2002	Mohammedia	MAR	Rudy McNeill	RSA	Dina Ramadan	EGY
2003	P. Elizabeth	RSA	Aaron Larkens	RSA	Philippa Baer	RSA
2005	Dar es Salaam	TAN	Ahmed Ragab	EGY	Emma Walker	RSA
2006	Alexandria	EGY	Ahmed Ragab	EGY	Mariem Zribi	TUN
2008	Grand Baie	MRI	Mohamed Benouali	ALG	Yannis Cherif	ALG

Development of Optimist sailing in Africa also featured strongly in IODA's training and development programmes as described elsewhere.

Caribbean

Development of Optimist sailing in the Caribbean in the 1990s has been briefly described in the account of the 1999 Worlds in Martinique. Following the stimulus of that Worlds and the millennium experience, further progress was rapid, including several new fleets. Until 1999 few if any Caribbean Optimist sailors had competed outside their region and in 1999 only one of the 25 Caribbean sailors had placed in the top half of the Worlds fleet. Now participation in the North Americans, and from 2002 the Worlds, increased and results improved.

By the 2006 Worlds eleven Caribbean sailors from seven different countries, now including representatives of the Dominican Republic and the Netherlands Antilles, placed in the top half. Matthew Scott from Trinidad had unexpectedly won the silver medal in 2005, and in 2008 Raúl Ríos of Puerto Rico and Ian Barrows of the USVI took gold and silver, with Puerto Rico taking the team racing title.

While the larger and wealthier countries unsurprisingly provided the most successful sailors in and after the Optimist, IODA also encouraged and in many cases sponsored the smaller fleets. As of 2007 IODA had 16 members in the region (just two less than ISAF) with fleets in, among others, Antigua, Bahamas, Cayman, El Salvador, Netherlands Antilles, St. Lucia and St. Vincent, and even in islands which cannot for various reasons be national members such as Anguilla and Carriacou.

The enthusiasm would extend to hosting the IODA North American Championship: Trinidad in 2005, Puerto Rico in 2006, Curaçao in 2008 and the Dominican Republic in 2009.

The possibility of some day qualifying for the Olympics is the dream motivating many Optimist sailors, and in the Caribbean this has come good. From this first generation to compete internationally have already come seven Olympians: Thomas Barrows, Cy Thompson and Mayumi Roller of the USVI, Juan I. Maegli from Guatemala, Andrew Lewis from Trinidad, Greg Douglas from Barbados (later Canada) and Philippine van Aanholt from the Netherlands Antilles. Results at the Youth Olympics and ISAF Youth Worlds suggest that others may achieve this goal in the coming years. As a bonus some of the first generation impressed on the U.S. InterCollegiate circuit and coaches began talent spotting in the region.

Oceania

This vast continent must be divided into three components: Australia, New Zealand and the South Pacific.

The most challenging of these areas is the South Pacific islands, separated by vast and expensive distances and mostly with individually small populations. There is the additional problem that the highest level of sailing is in the Francophone territories. Of these Tahiti is a member of ISAF and thus entitled to participate in IODA Worlds (and has done so since 1989) but New Caledonia is not. The latter however, as with all other French overseas territories, may compete in IODA continentals.

An Oceanian championship had been started in Rarotonga in the Cook Islands in 1997. IODA gave permission but had little input to the event. It was reported to have had 32 sailors from six 'countries'*. In 1999 (the event was planned to be biennial) an event was held in Fiji with 51 from eight countries, but since the boats used were not Class- or ISAF-legal it was not recognised by IODA.

In 2001 in Tahiti IODA became involved. Michel Barbier as an official of the French Sailing Federation could travel to what was legally part of France. Nine countries sent a total of 44 sailors and in these, the first detailed results now available, it is clear that only New Zealand could match the French; between them they took all ten top places. This time the boats were Class-legal: 12 were sold to the Cook Islands with '6 for 5' assistance from IODA, 8 to New Caledonia and 30 remained in Tahiti.

Successive championships were as follows:

2002	Samoa	52 sailors from 10 countries*		
2004	New Caledonia	37	do	7	do
2006	Cook Islands	21	do	7	do

* Note that New Caledonia, Tahiti and Wallis & Futuna are treated as countries.

New Zealand

The first complete team had appeared at the Worlds in 1991 when the NZL Yachting Federation had organised Optimist trials for the top sailors from the local P-Class and Starlings. President Hal Wagstaff had said "We have to ask whether we can afford to have our young people sailing in a vacuum". Participation proved controversial and the team next appeared in 1994. Members still intended to go on to sail the national P-Class but, unlike traditionally, they seem also to have sailed Optimists until 14 or 15. In 1996 local builder Keith Elliott was one of the first two manufacturers of the 'IOD95' and by 2000 had built over 150 boats.

It was clear from the start that the New Zealanders could sail. Indeed one of the team of 1996, Tom Ashley, went on to become the only known IODA Worlds participant to win Olympic gold at windsurfing. The new decade produced the next generation of Olympians including silver medallists Peter Burling and Carl Evans, and in the final year of this history the Kiwis produced the triumphs shown in the report of that year below.

Australia

Huge distances and several strong local Classes had delayed the spread of Optimists in Australia. In 2002 *Optiworld* announced breakthrough. The Australian Yachting Federation, under the influence of Ukrainian-born AYF head coach Victor Kovalenko, decided to recognise and promote the Optimist. "Optimist dinghies" wrote Victor " are the future of international junior sailing in Australia". He was supported by the 2000 Olympic gold medallist Belinda Stowell, a Zimbabwe-born ex-Optimist. In the same year a Sydney boatbuilder got approval to build.

It was something of a false start. The builder never got going and in 2005 sold his moulds. While the buyer, Steven Bond, got IODA approval to build, he decided instead to import boats from China. With a very commercial approach and further support from the AYF, sales took off. The Olympic gold medal won in 2008 by Elise Rechichi, a pioneer former Optimist sailor from Western Australia, did no harm either.

As of 2007 the Australians still had a way to go: their best place at the New Zealand Nationals was 38th/221. But looking ahead and outside the scope of this book, in the next five years nearly 1,000 sail numbers would be issued and at the latest Nationals 123 AUS boats participated . . . in Tasmania.

Arabian Gulf

The first Gulf state to join IODA was Kuwait which had bought some 40 Optimists after the devastation of the Gulf War. In 1996 they hosted a Pan-Arab Regatta but there was only one visiting sailor from the Gulf. The next breakthrough came in 1998, immediately after Dubai had hosted the ISAF World Sailing Championship and learned of the background of most of the participants. They were guided by Dubai-resident Australian Barrie Harmsworth. Despite a less than happy experience of premature participation in the millennium Worlds, the Dubai International Marine Club offered to host the 2001 IODA Asians. This stimulated interest from Abu Dhabi, Bahrain and Qatar: 13 Gulf sailors participated and, perhaps more importantly, the 110 charter boats imported for the event remained in the region. In 2002 IODA organised a coach-training course in Dubai, and Qatar initiated the first 'Sail the Gulf' regatta.

It must be said that progress thereafter until the end of the period in 2007 was slow. The waters of the Gulf are fantastic but seem to have been appreciated more by foreigners than nationals.

New members 2000-2007

In early 2000 there were 20 countries which at that time were members of ISAF but not of IODA. The *Optiworld* newsletter wondered: "No more world left?" By 2007 11 of them had joined, and IODA had found a few more:

2000	Barbados, Grenada, Moldova, St. Lucia, St. Vincent, Samoa
2001	Antigua, Bahrain, Kenya, Netherlands Antilles, Qatar
2002	American Samoa, El Salvador, Nicaragua, Papua New Guinea, Solomon I.
2003	Bahamas, Dominican Republic, Tanzania, Uganda
2005	*Serbia,* Vanuatu
2006	*Georgia,* Libya
2007	*Macedonia, Montenegro*

In Serbia Jasminka Lagator created in 2006 a South East European Optimist Cup (SEEOC) on Lake Palic which provided regional competition not only for the three new Balkan members but also Bulgaria, Hungary and Romania

Technical Administration

For the first three years of the decade Hans Thijsse had chaired this committee but Curly Morris returned in 2003.

In 2001 David Harte retired as prototype measurer. His importance in the establishment of the 'IOD95' one-design and hence in the history of IODA may be gauged by the tribute paid to him by president René Kluin:

> *"IODA should consider itself in debt forever with David: without him the development of the 'IOD95' would never have been a success. The way he knew to instruct new builders how to conquer difficulties and to correct mistakes - not as a policeman, but more as a goodwilling help - made him a very appreciated and respected representative of IODA, even later on when he was sent out to check the real production on consistency with the building approval."*

The position was filled by Luis Horta, who had been an IM since 1995 and, as a part-time postgraduate student, was ideally suited to undertake the ongoing work.

He developed a roll-up sail-measurement template which greatly eased that task, and continued in the position until the very end of the period.

Technical Matters 2000-2007

Foils

In 2002 the Technical Committee addressed the problem of foils. The two main objectives were to standardise the rudder to a shape which was efficient but reduced the benefit of 'sculling', and to reduce the price of both foils by banning wooden foils ("wood is an exotic material") on GRP boats and standardising the epoxy laminates.

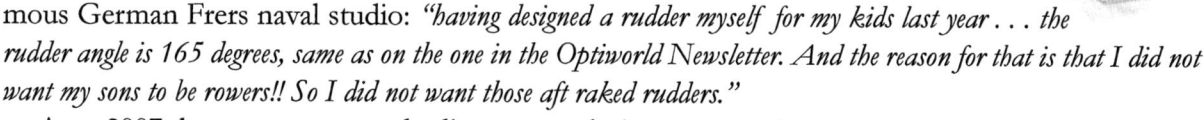

No more magic foils!

Intriguingly when the committee's design for the rudder was published, it received unexpected endorsement from Martín Billoch, world champion of 1974 and now a senior figure in the famous German Frers naval studio: *"having designed a rudder myself for my kids last year . . . the rudder angle is 165 degrees, same as on the one in the Optiworld Newsletter. And the reason for that is that I did not want my sons to be rowers!! So I did not want those aft raked rudders."*

As at 2007 the attempt to standardise on one-design seems to have been successful. At the Worlds at the end of 2006 over 80% of sailors were willing to accept the foils supplied with the (mandatory) charter hulls. Only a minority brought their own. However specialist manufacturers continued to claim that their products were superior and some distributors priced them accordingly, usually offering the alternative of cheaper foils which did not conform to the new Class Rules.

Sails

In 1993 the Technical Committee had taken action against ' throw-away' sails, specifying a minimum thickness of 0.15mm. However in 1999 or 2000 a new sailcloth appeared on the market. Variously known as 'sharkskin' or 'ripstop' it involved a weave with tiny squares too small to be measured non-destructively, i.e. without the risk of pushing the measuring device through the sail. It was believed that this cloth had a short life-span and it was even suspected that it enabled sailmakers to create sails which would stretch after first measurement. There were problems with establishing measurement criteria - the ISAF's Equipment Rules of Sailing seemed inadequate - and also with grandfathering. Only in 2004 was a satisfactory solution found.

In 2003 a further problem emerged. Sailmakers discovered an ambiguity in Class Rules - and again possibly in the Equipment Rules of Sailing - which allowed an extended roach. The dimensions of the extension grew and the sails came to be called 'dumbo' (after Mr. Disney's big-eared flying elephant). This time the Technical Committee found it easier to re-write the Class Rule and in August 2004 the AGM voted unanimously to ban such sails, without even grandfathering them as it was felt that they were too fragile to last anyway.

In March 2005 IODA investigated the possibility of introducing a one-design sail. Since it had no in-house sailmaking expertise it announced a competition open to sailmakers to design an 'IOD08' one design sail. In retrospect it was like the proverbial "asking turkeys to vote for Christmas". The leading sailmakers delighted in creativity, designing sails reputedly ever faster each year and offering different cuts for different weights so that as soon as a sailor gained a few kilos he/she had to buy a different one. There was almost no response to the competition idea and it was quietly dropped.

In fairness different cuts *were* best for different weights of sailor and this was a factor in enabling a wide range of weights and heights to sail the Optimist competitively, which does not seem to be the case of any other single-hander dinghy.

Maintaining the One-Design

Data from the Worlds of 2007 showed that the diversity of hulls used to qualify sailors was even more marked than the pattern which had emerged by 1999. Winner and Rio Tecna between them still represented 45% of the hulls used to qualify, but hulls from 18 other builders had been used. Almost all teams outside South America included sailors who had used a variety of hulls in which to qualify, confirming that no one now believed that one *had* to have a particular make of boat to do well.

Of course these data did not show total market share; for example only five U.S. sailors participate in the Worlds but the USA market could be as high as 1,000 boats a year. A notable feature of the period was the rapid expansion of building in China, including by joint-ventures between Chinese and European companies. The Registration Book always showed the true country of build.

The work of maintaining the integrity of the one-design remained important. The requirement that a prototype from each set of moulds be measured meant that there were the *"periodical inspections on the builder's premises"* recommended by the CBC back in 1992, as the major builders needed new or additional moulds. Sample hulls were also checked at most IODA events. In 2004 an unannounced inspection at the Garda Meeting detected boats from one builder weighing up to a kilo less than certified by the national measurer. Despite warnings, the MNA failed to control the practice and a year later, with underweight hulls still being incorrectly certified, IODA ceased to supply the builder with Registration Books.

Advertising

It emerged later that advertising was nor a matter for technical committees but it was in the Class Rules. In 1999-2002 advertising on equipment became a hot topic. Since the earliest days some Optimists had been sponsored - that was the whole basis of Major McKay's programme - but advertising had run into opposition in, for example, the early days in Finland. In the 1990s there was huge debate in the sport about future policy.

There were big differences even in the attitude of IODA member countries. This could lead for example to situations like the St. Thomas Regatta in the U.S. Virgins: US Sailing was hotly opposed to all advertising but the boats coming up from the grassroots programmes of the southern islands were smothered in it and large amounts of sticky tape had to be applied. There was the additional factor that IODA wanted to be able to offer 'clean' boats to important event sponsors such as Nesquik.

Sticky tape!

ISAF policy stated clearly: "ISAF Classes: Totally left to the sailors of all ISAF Class to decide to what level they want to allow advertising." After much debate IODA decided that the differences in philosophy between its members were so great that the only solution was to allow members to do as they wished in their home waters but to remove advertising when travelling abroad. The decision by each country would depend on agreement between the national Optimist association and its national sailing authority.

However this idea was not immediately acceptable to the ISAF and much negotiation was required before the final text was agreed as:

> *"As approved by the International Sailing Federation (ISAF), any National Owners Association with the consent of its Member National Authority (MNA) may permit full or restricted Category C for boats of that nation sailing in their national waters. Such advertising may relate to the ownership of the boat (i.e. may be restricted to club owned boats etc. only)."*

This was by no means a perfect solution. There was not much problem at IODA events where the relatively small number of boats on national teams could be stripped of any advertising (not forgetting that outside Europe most teams used charter boats). But at other regattas there were problems; for example at the Easter Meeting on Garda the Italians, who did not permit advertising, objected to that carried by, for example, the Danes. A certain amount of eye-closing may have been necessary.

Regatta Committee

In 2000 Michel Barbier was obliged to retire under the 10-year rule and the chair was taken by Kenneth Andreasen, who was later to be head coach of the US Sailing Olympic squad. Michel returned in 2002 only to retire permanently in 2005 when he 'emigrated' to Martinique, the home of his new wife Mireille (whom he had met at the Worlds of 1999). He was sadly missed as he had served IODA since 1981, but two excellent IROs had been recruited, Alen Kustic (CRO) in 2002 and Luis Ormaechea (ESP) in 2003. The latter became chair of the committee. Nazli Imre, who had been responsible for the shoreside part of the work retired in 2003; no satisfactory replacement could be found and in 2005 Amneris Calle de Cloos, who had done an excellent job in Salinas the previous year, was hired as part-time regatta secretary to undertake some of the work.

Regattas 2000-2007

The 'Miami Herald' mentioned below is the trophy for the aggregate results of the best four sailors from a country. In a period of rapidly developing fleets it is a good measure of the relative strength of the teams each year.

2000 LA CORUÑA, SPAIN   *252 SAILORS FROM 59 COUNTRIES*

The opportunities, problems and lessons of the biggest Worlds have been described elsewhere.

Ashore the huge dinghy park occupied a whole wing of the old harbour and the atmosphere was great, but abnormal Atlantic weather fronts limited racing to just ten races.

On the water it was Croatia's year. After Dario Kliba's bronze in 1995 the country had gained silver, through Aron Lolic in 1996 and Tonci Stipanovic in 1999. Now Sime Fantela, who had been third in 1998 aged 12, won personal gold and led his team to top place in the Miami Herald. Placed fifth was Igor Marenic who was to be Sime's long-term 470 crew. Twelve years later they were to be faced with the 2000 silver medallist, Argentinian Lucas Calabrese, in the medal race at the 2012 Olympics; Sime and Igor won the race, but Lucas took the Olympic bronze.

2001 QINGDAO, CHINA   208 SAILORS FROM 44 COUNTRIES

If there is good wind at a regatta not much else matters: if there is little wind everything does. Qingdao was already in the running to host the sailing events of the 2008 Olympics and indeed was confirmed as such during this event. The Optimist experience in 2001 would lead to frantic but ultimately futile attempts to get the venue changed. Despite the best efforts of Michel Barbier and his race management team, it was only possible to run seven of the scheduled 15 races and the team-racing event was held without repechage; Argentina won anyway.

Sitting around on a hot airless beach led to endless complaints, even one that the big beach parasols advertised the famous local beer (in Chinese) contrary to the ban on alcohol advertising at junior events. Fortunately Nazli Imre on behalf of IODA and Meng Shuxia for the Chinese Y.A. made the best of the situation. The hotel was well air-conditioned and the food a big improvement on the previous year.

The results were thought at the time to be distorted in favour of the light-wind sailors from Asia. Few at the time realised that Asian sailing was on the rise: fifth placed Teo Wee Chin was to win Sin-

gapore's first ISAF Youth Worlds gold in 2005, and 11th over-all was future Olympic champion Lija Xu. And the winner in the end of this "infamous" Worlds was the silver medallist from the previous year, Lucas Calabrese.

2002 CORPUS CHRISTI, U.S.A. 208 SAILORS FROM 46 COUNTRIES

Corpus Christi on the Gulf of Mexico was supposed to be one of the windiest USA venues. It was windy . . . on the practice day and the rest day. Otherwise the wind struggled to reach 12 knots but the full programme was sailed.

The opening ceremony was held on 4th of July and merged with celebrations of the national holiday. This included the presentation of tiny children dressed in US military and service uniforms with much patriotic music. Some adults held their breath at the reaction of teams such as the Chinese but they didn't seem to notice: maybe they were used to such displays at home.

Filip Matika of Croatia became at the age of 11 years 10 months the youngest champion on record by a decisive 46 points over his compatriot Stjepan Cesic. Filip was to win in 2003 also and later become world Laser 4.7 champion and Radial silver medallist.

A fascinating battle for the girls' prize took place between two future Olympic medallists, Lijia Xu, now at her fourth Worlds and 1m70/54kg, and Hannah Mills of Great Britain at 1m53/40kg. Tension mounted as both sailors had OCSs in later races but Lijia finally won out with 6th over-all as against Hannah's 9th.

Asian sailors showed that Qingdao had not been that exceptional, taking four of the top 20 places, and China won bronze in the team-racing.

2003 GRAN CANARÍA, SPAIN   221 SAILORS FROM 50 COUNTRIES

One of the great yacht clubs of the world with a long and successful Optimist history welcomed IODA back after hosting a highly successful Europeans in 2001. At last there was decent wind, rising to 15-20 knots for most races.

Filip Matika retained his title with little difficulty, scoring in single figures for 12 of the 15 races. Second was Jesse Kirkland of Bermuda sailing in his fifth successive Worlds (he had come 161st aged

11) and from a family largely responsible for reviving Optimist sailing in that country in 1998. With brother Zan he was to qualify for the 49er event in 2012.

Hannah Mills was expected to be a certain winner of the girls' prize but had to carry a BFD and an OCS from the first half of racing. Since only two discards were applicable she had to sail carefully thereafter but did so to place 5th over-all. As often happens, one great sailor can inspire a team and GBR with two more sailors in the top 12 placed second in the Miami Herald, by far their best placing ever.

Argentina won the team-racing for the fourth successive year.

2004 SALINAS, ECUADOR   228 SAILORS FROM 51 COUNTRIES

Salinas may not be as well-known as Gran Canaría but its superb facilities were very similar. Sailing conditions were excellent with consistent 12-16 knots but most unusual in that this was under permanent 100% cloud cover.

Four years after many had scoffed at the 'freak' Asian results of Qingdao, that continent produced

the first Asian world champion in the person of Wei Ni from China. There was no disputing his win, by 47 points to 78 and with single figure results in all his 13 scoring races.

The other revelation of this championship was the arrival in the big time of New Zealand. Thirteen years after Hal Wagstaff had promoted participation, 14-year old Paul Snow-Hansen, who had scarcely been born at the time but had already achieved his country's best ever place to date with 24th in 2003, took the silver medal and his future 470 crew Dan Willcox came 4th. The team, which included future Olympians Carl Evans (silver in 2012), Snow-Hansen and Susannah Pyatt, took the Miami Herald Trophy for best team.

The team-racing was won by Poland, breaking an eight-year South American monopoly. The team included future Olympians Lukasz Przybytek and Kacper Zieminski.

2005 ST. MORITZ, SWITZERLAND 241 SAILORS FROM 52 COUNTRIES

Good 'Majola' thermal winds on the Silvaplana produced some fantastic racing, even if the coaches did not much enjoy fighting it out on bicycles along the shore of the lake. The jury too had problems in keeping up with the fleet in their ecologically correct power- (what power?) boats.

Tina Lutz of Germany was a very popular winner with all her scoring results in the top 10 and, like Hannah in 2003, inspired her team to win the Miami Herald, again for the first time ever. The top three Germans were all lake sailors from the Starnbergersee but any suggestion that sea-sailors could not do well was contradicted by the silver medal taken by Matthew Scott from Trinidad. Wu Jianan of China took bronze.

Wind was not helpful for the team-racing which took place on the arena-style lake in the centre of St. Moritz. Though it is famed as a match-racing venue, the wind failed to oblige on the scheduled day and was ultra-light on the rest-day used. Argentina regained their title but the light winds allowed a well-organised Malaysian team into silver.

Prizes were awarded by the great Jochen Schümann who cannot have expected to be awarding gold medals to the first ever of his compatriots to win them.

2006 MONTEVIDEO, URUGUAY 228 SAILORS FROM 50 COUNTRIES

The huge turnout for a 'Christmas Worlds' in South America showed how much the Optimist world had changed since the 133 sailors from 29 countries of 1992. The top ten teams were now from five continents rather than just South America versus Europe. Winds were generally good and local knowledge seemed to give no advantage.

For much of the regatta it looked as if a girl would win again in the person of Griselda Khng of Singapore, but in the final race Germany's Julian Autenrieth registered a 6th against Griselda's 10th to take the title by just two points. However Singapore won both the team-racing - beating traditional finalists Peru - and the Miami Herald.

2006 was a good year for girls with Stephanie Zimmermann (Peru) and Rufina Tan (Malaysia) in 4th and 5th places behind Griselda.

2007 CAGLIARI, ITALY 251 SAILORS FROM 55 COUNTRIES

The return to Europe set another new record for 'normal' Worlds. In fact since the 2006 event had extended to 2007, a total of 62 countries participated in the two Worlds of the year.

Conditions again were generally good and 13 races were sailed. New Zealand were back to even better than their 2004 form, taking gold through Chris Steele, bronze and best girl through Alex Maloney, and for the second time the Miami Herald. Reigning champion Julian Autenrieth was fourth, a poor last race leaving him just five points adrift. Greece rather unexpectedly won the team-racing.

Silver medallist Benjamin Grez of Chile was to go on to become one of the youngest sailors to qualify for the 2012 Olympics, but Chris Steele is perhaps the first champion to face up to the realities of modern sailing by looking directly to match-racing: *"I want to make a living at sailing. I enjoy match racing so that's a big factor at looking at the America's Cup. Since I was 14 I wanted to go down the America's Cup path."* He will be following a well-established tradition of ex-Optimist America's Cup heroes which includes Ed Baird, Dean Barker and Jordi Calafat. Alex Maloney is taking a more conventional route: having taken silver in the 2010 29er event at the ISAF Youth Worlds she was selected to test possible new Olympic skiffs and won the first ever Sailing World Cup event in the boat chosen for 2016, the 49erXX.

Miami Herald Summary 2000-2007

Results for this 'strongest team' trophy showed clearly the widening range of countries which could do well at the top level:

2000	Croatia	Italy	Argentina	2004	New Zealand	Poland	Italy
2001	Argentina	China	Spain	2005	Germany	Sweden	Peru
2002	Italy	Croatia	Argentina	2006	Singapore	Ecuador	Argentina
2003	Croatia	Great Britain	Argentina	2007	New Zealand	France	Italy

Continental Championships

The new Africans and Oceanians are described elsewhere. Detailed results of the championships of the new century are available on the IODA website, so the following describes trends.

Europeans

Numbers, which had shown little growth in the 1990s, started to grow again from 2002 due primarily to greater participation by East Europeans. By 2003 the Regatta Committee noted that race officers had to try to manage starts of 90 and 105 respectively, using three successive starts (two for boys, one for girls). They felt that these numbers were becoming unmanageable and pointed out that the ISAF recommendation was for not more than 80 boats on a start line. European members were reluctant to exclude non-Europeans, not least because they feared that they might thus be excluded from the two American continental championships. The compromise - accepted by 7 votes to 6 with 2 abstentions - was reached that European teams would be reduced to seven sailors (with at least three of each gender) and non-Europeans to a maximum team of four sailors (with at least one sailor of each gender). The effect on numbers was as follows:

	1999	2003	2007	
"West European"	168	168	143	
"East European"*	42	79	57	* Former Comecon & Yugoslavia.
Non-European	22	36	29	
	232	285	229	
(Girls)	(85)	(105)	(86)	

Thus the new quotas had, for the time being at least, resolved the startline problem, though it was reduced the number of non-European girls.

North Americans

In 1999 it had been agreed to limit entries to national teams, albeit of varying sizes due to the disparity of population. Huge open fleets such as the 145 USA sailors in 1995 did not allow the quality of racing now expected of an IODA continental championship. And in both the North and South American championships there were many more national teams, mostly from the Caribbean, wanting to participate.

The remarkable feature of the period was the emergence of first Bermudan, then Caribbean sailors as event winners, previously and understandably a USA virtual monopoly.

2000	T.J.Tullo*	USA	2004	Elijah Simmons*	BER
2001	T.J.Tullo	USA	2005	Colin Smith	USA
2002	Jesse Kirkland*	BER	2006	Ivan Aponte	PUR
2003	Sean Bouchard*	BER	2007	Raúl Ríos*	PUR

and in the final year Nikki Barnes (ISV) became the first islander to win the girls' prize.
* = Open winner. Others are first North American.

The size of the USA team was reduced . . . somewhat!

South Americans

The change in the leader board of the South Americans was also remarkable. Argentina, which had monopolised totally the championship in the 1990s, was challenged:

	Boys		Girls	
2000	Gustavo Mascarenhas*	BRA	Andrea Borges*	BRA
2001	Bernardo Luz	BRA	Maria Agustina Torre	ARG
2002	Enrique Haddad*	BRA	Maria Pía Benavides*	PER
2003	Tomás Agrimbau*	ARG	Victoria Travascio*	ARG
2004	Edgar Diminich*	ECU	Daniella Zimmermann*	PER
2005	Alex Zimmermann	PER	Maria José Cucalon*	ECU
2006	Jonathan Martinetti	ECU	Arianna Villena	ECU
2007	Benjamin Grez	CHI	Stephanie Zimmermann	PER

* = Open winner. Others are first South American.

Asians

The main feature of the Asian Championship in this period was the excellent performances by girls. The placing of the first girl was as follows:

2000	Nurul Ain	MAS	3
2001	Yoko Kiuchi	JPN	12
2002	Lian Cuixian	CHN	2
2003	Griselda Khng	SIN	3
2004	Wu Tong	CHN	9
2005	Jovina Chu	SIN	2
2006	Griselda Khng	SIN	2
2007	Rachel Lee	SIN	2

Griselda

Other Regattas

The appetite for 'unofficial' regattas, usually with no qualification required, continued to expand. Easter had for years seen a mass migration and in 2007 it was calculated that 1,630 sailors from 48 countries sailed in international events on the same day. The biggest of them, the 'Easter Meeting' in Italy is in the Guinness Book of Records as the largest single-Class regatta in the world.

Now all winter there seemed to be regattas in the (optimistically) warmer south of Europe at every school break, such as the St, Nicholas in Croatia, the Euromed in Malta, the Campobasso in Naples and several in Spain at venues such as Palamos, Palma and Vigo. Likewise in the summer many national championships saw increasing numbers of foreign entries.

Team racing in Europe was increasingly popular and well served. The Europa Team Cup sailed on the Wannsee near Berlin had originated in 1987 and the Trofeo Rizzotti on Venice Lagoon had become international in 1996 under the influence of the late Giorgio Lauro, one of IODA's favourite IJs. Both of these were open to a mix of teams, national, provincial or club. In 2002 Lake Ledro in northern Italy initiated the GrandOptical Challenge Cup for European clubs. This was intended to stimulate inter-club team racing at national level, since each team had to have won a national inter-club championship. It was a great success but, perhaps regrettably, was to be replaced by a European inter-national team racing championship in 2008.

Chapter 9: Girls

Promoting women in sport is a subject on which much ink, paper and conference time have been expended. IODA has adopted a pragmatic approach.

Cliff McKay Jr. has clear memories that girls joined in the earliest fleets in Florida and Viggo is quoted in his retirement comments in 1981 that he wished he could have done more to promote girls' sailing. But the fact was that until the mid-1980s very few (in Europe less than ten) female sailors gained selection for national teams.

1985 Worlds: only 11 girls

Worlds or Europeans?

The main decisions which would shape IODA policies about girls were made in 1985-7. By a series of different decisions Optimist girls acquired two targets. They could either qualify for the Worlds and race against the boys, or they could compete for the reserved places in a girls-only fleets at the Europeans (which were, at least from 1988, open to non-European sailors).

The creation of an IODA European championship in 1983 led by 1985 to the decision that girls and boys at that event would race in separate fleets and that at least two of the seven places per nation (28.5%) would be reserved for girls - increased to three of eight (37.5%) in 1987. In 1986 the IODA AGM debated whether the Worlds too should have gender quotas and a split fleet. Two motions were debated: to add two places reserved for girls to the five-sailor national teams, or alternatively to reserve one place of the existing five for a girl. Both were rejected, not least because the female sailors present were emphatic that they wanted the chance to qualify in competition with boys and, having done so, wanted to sail against them at the Worlds.

The following year that decision was vindicated. Sabrina Landi of Italy, one of the girls who had influenced the 1986 decision (in 62nd place that year) shocked everyone by winning the 1987 Worlds outright. Never again was there much support for a separate girls' fleet at the Worlds.

Increasing numbers

From 1989 the number of girls qualifying for the Worlds began to increase. From an average of less than ten sailors, 7% of the fleet, in the 1980s it grew to an average for the 1990s of 13%. The main reason is probably that more girls entered national trials in view of the certainty, at least in Europe and other countries sending teams to the Europeans, that female participants would qualify for *something*. Other reasons for the increase may have been:

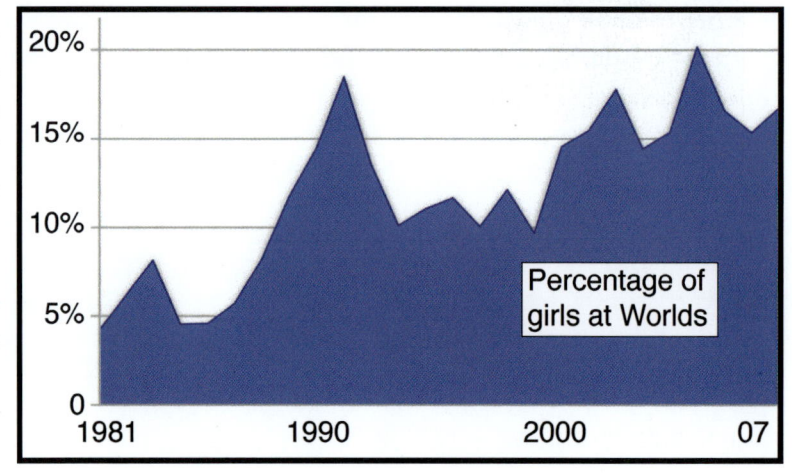

Percentage of girls at Worlds

- the introduction of womens' sailing (technically, events reserved for females) to the Olympics in 1988 though it was 1990 before the IYRU introduced girls' events to its Youth Worlds
- Sabrina's example. A girl *could* win, though it was nine years before another one did. However in 1991 there were for the first time two girls in the top ten and in 1993 another Italian, Claudia Tosi, did take bronze. In 1996 future Olympic medallist Lisa Westerhof of the Netherlands became the second girl to win gold.

Improved results

In the old century only two girls had won the open championship and in the '90s the average place of the best girl was 16th. In 2002 there was a sudden change, not in the percentage of girls present which rose only slightly to around 16%, but in the ranking of the best girl:

2002	6th	Lijia Xu	China
2003	5th	Hannah Mills	Great Britain
2004	12th	Tina Lutz	Germany
2005	1st	Tina Lutz	Germany
2006	2nd	Griselda Khng	Singapore
2007	3rd	Alex Maloney	New Zealand

The later dominance of Asian girls is outside the scope of this chronicle though, like other national or regional phenomena over the years, it is likely to be temporary.

A similar though less emphatic improvement can be seen in the results of the South American Championship. Whereas in the period 1995 to 2001 it had been rare to have a South American girl in the top ten places, in 2002-2007 a girl achieved such a place every year. There was little such improvement in the North American Championship results: in fact only one North American girl, Stephanie Roble (USA), achieved a top-ten placing in the period.

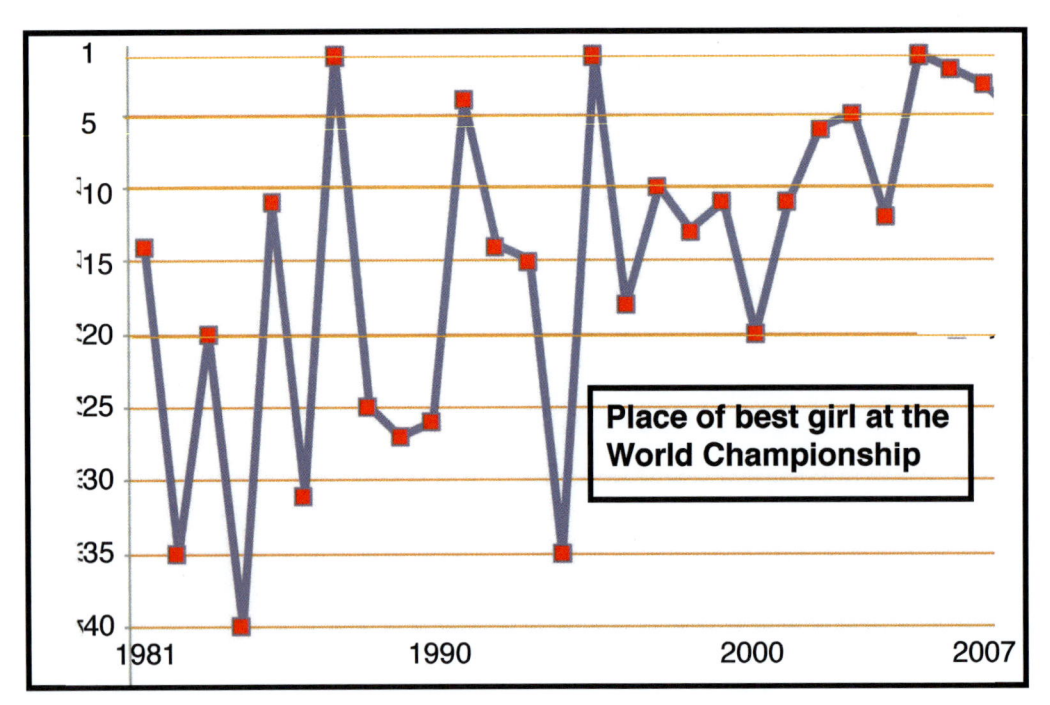

Quotas

The subject of quotas for female participation is a difficult one with, as with advertising, very diverse opinions in different parts of the world. IODA is a democratic organisation (one vote per country and a non-voting Executive) and decisions have to reflect often divergent views.

Girls' participation in the European Championship had continued satisfactorily, with most countries entering at least the three sailors prescribed. In 2003, when the total entry per nation was reduced to seven sailors to prevent the event becoming unmanageable, it was agreed to increase the proportional quota per gender to ensure at least three of the seven (43%) were girls. However at the same time and for the same reason, the total quota for non-Europeans was reduced to four with a minimum of only one girl. This reduced the number of non-European girls (and indeed the total number of non-European teams) and hence the opportunities for girls from those continents to compete at inter-continental level. For example future Olympic medallist Fernanda Oliveira (BRA) had won the 1996 *European* open championship.

There was no problem in Asia where, probably under the influence of the prestigious Asian Games, girls had always been prominent.

However opportunities to participate in the two American championships were not specified and in fact the level of female participation, despite the improvement in girls' results at the South Americans, remained low. In 2007 the AGM, after much negotiation with some Americans who disapproved of gender quotas, resolved that, except for very small teams, the following quotas would apply globally:

| Europeans: | 43% | North Americans: | 25% | Africans: | 27% |
| Asians: | 35% | South Americans | 25% | | |

This reflected the compromises with the continents concerned but at least there were now minimum quotas. It is interesting to compare the (de facto) women's quota of 34.5% at the 2008 Olympics.

The general subject of girls' sailing is too wide for this present work but it is interesting to note that at the massive Garda Easter Meeting, with up to a thousand sailors participating and no question of selection or qualification, the percentage of girls remains at around 30%.

After the Optimist

Whether or not women's Olympic events stimulated girls' Optimist sailing, a high proportion of female Olympic sailors now have an Optimist background. In 2012 the percentage of skippers who had sailed Optimists and had sailed them internationally was as follows:

	Sailed Optimists	Sailed Optimists Internationally
Laser Radial	78%	46%
470	95%	90%
Elliott MR	83%	25%

Although fewer Radial sailors had sailed internationally, those who had included all three medallists.

A longer term view of the link between Optimist and Olympic female sailors is shown below: (Regular = former Optimist sailor; **bold** = former IODA championship sailor)

		Gold	*Silver*	*Bronze*
1988	470	Allison Jolly	Marit Söderström	
1992	Europe	Linda Andersen	**Natalia Via Dufresne**	Julia Trotman
	470	Theresa Zabell		
1996	Europe	Kristine Roug	**Margriet Matthijsse**	
	470	Theresa Zabell	Yumiko Shige	
2000	Europe		**Margriet Matthijsse**	**Serena Amato**
	470	Belinda Stowell		
2004	Europe	**Siren Sundy**		Signe Livbjerg
	470	**Sofia Bekatorou**	**Natalia Via Dufresne**	**Therese Torgersson**
2008	Radial	Anna Tunnicliffe	**Gintare Volungeviciute**	**Lijia Xu**
	470	Elise Rechichi	**Marcelien de Koning**	**Fernanda Oliveira**
	Yngling	Sarah Ayton	**Mandy Mulder**	**Sofia Bekatorou**
2012	Radial	**Lijia Xu**	**Marit Bouwmeester**	**Evi van Acker**
	470		**Hannah Mills**	**Lisa Westerhof**
	MR	Tamara Echegoyen		**Silja Lehtinen**

Only skippers are noted above but **Lobke Berkhout** who won the 1994 Europeans went on to two Olympic medals as crew.

Not just girls

The foundation and early years of IODA owed much to Edith Jacobsen. Born in northern England she was much more than just Viggo's secretary and had considerable input, especially during his pre-regatta and regatta visits, sharing his pragmatic approach. Hanne Rix, who followed her as secretary of IODA, combined great secretarial skills with a passion for sailing she shared with husband Torben.

In the same tradition the Optimist Class has, since 1982, succeeded in attracting outstanding women into its administration.

Helen Mary, the first woman elected in IODA, to the Regatta Committee in that year, served thereafter as vice-president, president and president of honour. In the IYRU she became in 1990 only the second woman to join a multi-gender committee, the all-important CPOC, and in 1994 was the first woman to be *elected* to any non-gender-specific position, vice-chair of the International Classes. She is also the only female member of the Irish Sailing Association's 'Hall of Fame' and in 2008 the first female recipient of the ISAF Development Award.

While never reserving places for women, IODA had a female vice-president for thirteen of the fifteen years 1992-2007 in the persons of Gudrun von Dahl (GER) and Mimi Santos (POR) as well as, more recently, future ISAF vice-president Nazli Imre (TUR) on the Regatta Committee and Hyo Kyung Jang (KOR) on the Technical Committee (and the first ever female ISAF International Measurer).

IODA also tried to have at least one female on its juries, most notably Barbara Farquhar IJ, IU (USA), a member of the ISAF Review Board, who frequently chaired them.

Chapter 10: Training & Development

While the primary objective of IODA is to provide racing for young people at low cost by administering the Class Rules and supervising its championships, it is also charged with "co-ordinating youth work between member countries" and this has led to some involvement with training and development in member countries new to the Class.

Prior to the allocation of funds from the sail button in 1989, any training activity tended to be on a self-financing basis, primarily promoting contact between coaches from the more 'developed' members and the newer ones. Jes Retbøll in particular was involved in this, working especially with Al Chandler and Ng Ser Miang.

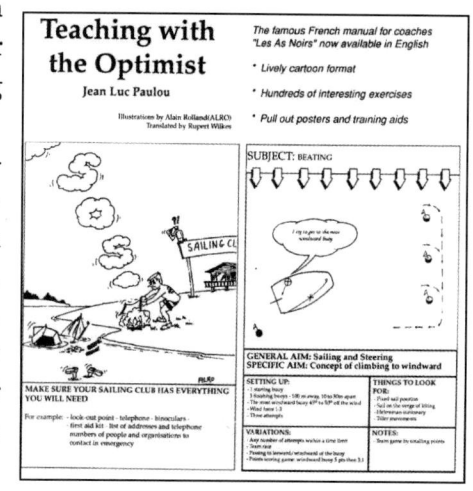

IODA also produced some training material, notably *Optimist World I* written by Jes, and *Teaching with the Optimist* (translated by the Wilkes's son Rupert, with FFV permission, from Jean Luc Paulou's brilliant *Les As Noirs* instructors' manual). Videos were produced by Jes and later by Norman Jenkins. IODA also publicised the increasing number of commercially available books such as Phil Slater's *Optimist Racing*, *The Winner's Guide to Optimist Sailing* published in 1997 by Gary Jobson & Jay Kehoe, and similar works in other languages.

The 1990s

Courses were partly financed by the sail button revenue but considerable help was received from the IYRU World Youth Sailing Trust, at that time a fairly autonomous trust funded by a number of wealthy sailors and administered by Israeli Julius Blankstein until his sad death in 2000. It is also believed that Al and Ser Miang provided additional aid.

Between 1990 and 1994 the main beneficiaries were in Asia. Four courses were held, attended by instructors from nine countries. In 1995-6 Nesquik sponsorship enabled a wider programme of courses, seven in those two years and a further eight before the end of the decade. The main beneficiaries were in the Caribbean and in Eastern Europe. The latter may seem strange but there was a big need to train up amateur and semi-professional instructors to replace the state-funded coaches of the communist era. There were also some special cases such as Malta, just starting in Optimists, and New Zealand where they knew a lot about sailing but had little experience of how to rig and sail the modern Optimists they were introducing.

The objective of IODA throughout was to train instructors, not the current generation of sailors.

2000-2007

In the new millennium the explosion of Optimist sailing in the Caribbean and in Africa led to concentration on those two regions. In these regions it was often possible to hold multi-country courses but it was also necessary to provide some individual courses elsewhere. Eastern Europe was not forgotten and in fact the last course of the period helped to revive the fleet in Serbia.

In 2001 IODA introduced its '6 for 5' scheme. Countries seeking to start or enlarge Optimist fleets could apply for one free boat for every five bought. The boats could be bought from any approved builder and several builders offered very special prices for IODA-sponsored purchases. All the boats had to be owned by an association, club or other 'not-for-profit' organisation, and be available to introduce the children of non-sailors to the sport. Consideration was also given to supplying sails and rigs for locally-built wood/epoxy Optimists. The equipment was generally supplied directly from the builder and was with basic level sails and foils.

More than 270 Optimists had been sponsored by the end of the period. The 26 beneficiaries were:

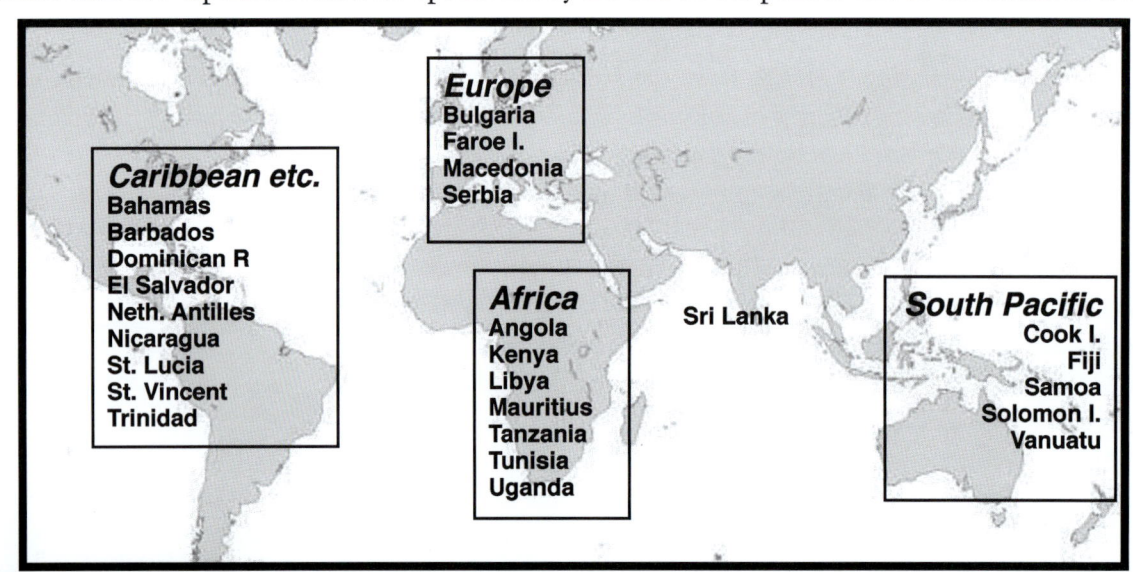

Since most of the countries helped were geographically fairly isolated it was possible for national associations to bar 'go faster' gear (they would charter when travelling). On this basis it was usually possible to supply the new fleets with Optimists at under $1,500 each and in several cases governments were persuaded to waive import duties and sales taxes.

Following on from the free entries and charter given in 1999 and 2000, participation grants were subsequently given to other countries sending sailors to continental or regional events for the first time. While this was an incentive for the sailors from the new fleets, it also gave the accompanying team-leaders the chance to learn about best-practice and to make contacts.

While not officially part of the IODA development programme, much informal transfer of experience resulted from the subsidised practice of sending to continental regattas an ISAF-qualified Race Officer and an International Measurer, as well as the relevant IODA vice-president. Juries too were selected with great care to promote consistent interpretation of the Rules and to show how best to introduce rule observance.

Chapter 11: How many Optimists?

There is much speculation (not to say some wild guesses) as to how many Optimists have been built.

The following is an attempt to analyse this, and what have been the trends in sales.

1980 Survey

Data for the early period are confused and were so even at the time. Prior to 1973 the only information comes from *Reports from Member Associations 1979-80* (though some of the reports are from as early as 1975). Members were asked how many 'registered' Optimists they had. There was much confusion as to what 'registered' meant, but the best available answers combined to equal around 70,000 boats. Since 43,000 plaques had been issued since 1973, it was assumed that some 27,000 pre-dated that date. Moreover the same countries reported at least 15,000 *unregistered* boats and, as Viggo commented, "to this can be added an unknown number in several countries which are without contact to IODA". It later emerged that there must have been thousands in the USSR and the Comecon countries. Someone at the 1981 AGM estimated the total of all boats as 140,000 but that, as Viggo commented, "is esteemed to be rather high".

However plaque figures for the period 1973-1980 are not necessarily valid evidence for the number of boats built. Before 1996 plaques were issued to national Optimist or national sailing associations. The procedure was that then "the owner or builder shall apply to the appropriate National [Sailing] Authority for a sail number" and *subsequently* have the boat measured. But in the days of wooden boats there is strong evidence that, for many plaques, no sail number was applied for, no boat was ever measured, and even that boats were never built. For example in 1979:
- In Britain, a typical batch of 100 plaques 38201-38300 was bought in that year: only 20 of them were ever measured, almost all built by known builders. For the others there is no evidence that the buyer ever applied for a sail number or indeed that the boats were ever built.
- Italy reported: "Up to June 1st 1979 only 885 dinghies were regularly registered compared to 1357 assigned sail numbers."

Of the 70,000 'registered' Optimists reported in 1980, over 67% were reported by the four Scandinavian countries (34,100) and France (12,700). But few of these were measured Optimists; Sweden reported 16,000 registered but only 3,600 measured, Norway 1,850 and 300. Of course the Scandinavian countries had started early and there is no question that there had been a massive amount of building, but many of the figures may reflect every boat ever built, regardless of whether or not it was still sailing.

Plaque Sales 1980-1989

The number of IYRU/ISAF plaques issued fell sharply after around 1980, from around 5,700 a year in 1973-80 to around 3,550 in the next decade. It is believed that the main reasons are that most hulls were now made from the more durable GRP and that they were built by commercial companies which were much more likely to use all the plaques they bought.

From 1981, score-sheets from the Worlds have survived and comparing the most recent sail number presented is, for most countries, the most reliable indication of the increase in the number of

Optimists in that country. It is believed that in general sail numbers were now only being issued to boats which had plaques, though there is some doubt as to whether this was true in France.

Plaque Sales 1990-1998

Plaque sales in this nine year period fell around 12%, from 32,000 to 28,300. The main reason seems to have been the decline of sales to France by nearly 4,000 and to Scandinavia by nearly 5,000, which was only partly counteracted by sales to the USA increasing by around 5,000.

The decline in France seems to have been very largely due to the fact that plaques and sail-numbers were less often issued to non-legal sailing school boats, which already in 1992 accounted for over 60% of purchases; certainly no plaques were issued for such boats after 1995.

The decline in Scandinavia is more difficult to explain. Certainly in 1992 Denmark reported a 20% reduction in the number of sailors over the previous four years, and Finland and Norway reported nil growth. This may be related to the fall in population of Optimist age (Denmark actually experienced negative population growth in the early 1980s) but it is also possible that the large number of good secondhand GRP boats, following the boom in sales of Scandinavian-built Falsleds and Winners, reduced the market for new boats. Statistics shown below for Laser sales suggest that there may come a saturation point for sales of new boats.

Plaque Sales 1999-2007

Total sales rose from 28,300 to 33,250 in the nine years. A further decline in sail numbers issued in France (which probably also reflected an actual decline in the number of sailors) was balanced by a corresponding increase in the USA.

Many traditional markets such as Italy, Germany and Great Britain showed substantial growth and even Scandinavia saw a modest increase, but the main increases came primarily from Asia and Eastern Europe. This undoubted growth in Asia (excluding Japan) is difficult to measure because, perhaps for cultural reasons, few countries issue sequential numbers. Xtreme Sailboats in Singapore built around 1,400 in the period which almost all certainly remained in Asia. It is unknown how many of the thousands of Optimists built in China were for export to other continents but they included 700 bought by the city of Qingdao in preparation for the legacy of the Olympics. Participation in the Nationals of other countries, such as Malaysia 140, Thailand 108, Taipei 80 and Hong Kong 60, indicates strong growth, while Praga Marine in India built over 150.

In Eastern Europe the strongest growth seems to have been in Poland and former Yugoslavia (not least as a higher proportion now carried plaques), but the giant Russian market was only just beginning to open up.

'Saturation'

To summarise the plaque figures shown above, the pattern had been:

	Total	Average per year	
1973-1980	43,000	5,733	(average of 7.1/2 years)
1981-1989	32,000	3,555	
1990-1998	28,281	3,142	
1999-2007	33,252	3,695	

While the many factors which may have influenced this pattern have been discussed above, it is difficult to estimate the influence of 'saturation', the tendency of enough good secondhand boats to reduce demand for new ones (as I write, I have found a 13 year old Winner boat for sale, described as "a good tidy racing Optimist which is perfect to get children into competitive racing").

In this context it is interesting to compare sail numbers issued in the Laser Class, the only other dinghy Class remotely similar in size to the Optimist:

	Latest Sail Number	Issued in Period	Per Year	Notes
1980	86490	86390	8,639	Launched in 1971 with sail number 100
1989	142789	56,299	6,255	
1998	166270	23,481	2,609	
2006*	188575	22,305	2,788	* 2007 figure not available.

Data from http://www.abclubhk.com/download/LaserBoatAge.pdf

Durability

As has been noted above, modern GRP Optimists appear to have a long life, passing from top-level competition to local competition to use by novices. IODA even had to pass a Class Rule in 2006 permitting legal hulls built in 1992 or earlier to race without producing measurement certificates.

At top level, hulls are generally used for at least four years. In 2000 IODA investigated the age of hulls (excluding charter) used at the European championship. It found the following:

Build Year	
2000	18%
1999	27%
1998	27%
1997	17%
Older	11%

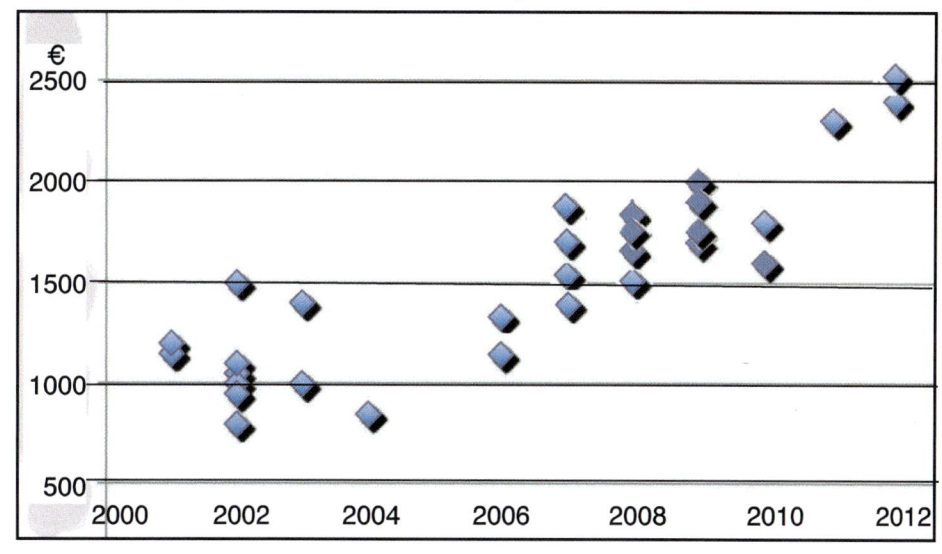

(Curiously the oldest boats were not from the poorest countries but used by freshwater sailors.)

This durability is reflected in secondhand prices. An indication of these, from after the period of this history but indicative of relative values, is taken from the price of boats advertised on the German DODV website in May 2013. Note that these prices include German sales tax which is currently 19%, and additional equipment such as trolleys and covers.

The cost of ownership was therefore around €150-250 per year.

Chapter 12: The Optimist and the Olympics

Pierre de Coubertin wrote:

"Olympism seeks to create a way of life based on the joy found in effort".

This could be taken as the mission statement of the Optimist. As Major McKay wrote:

"the character building aspects are better realized when competition is involved".

The Olympic dream is not for all. A study of the sailors who had taken part in the Optimist Worlds of 1994 showed that only around 15% of them had taken part in trials for the Games, only 9% qualified and only three individuals won medals. Most, 69% in the developed countries of the E.U and 52% elsewhere, continued sailing outside the Olympic framework.

Nevertheless the link between the Optimist and the Olympics is important, primarily to help the Games to "inspire a generation" but also to convince sports authorities worldwide to invest in junior sailing.

In the final year of this survey the International Olympic Committee decided to introduce a Youth Olympic Games. Sailing chose to be included and opted for the age category of 15-16, using the Byte dinghy. To no-one's surprise 87% of the qualifiers in the dinghy section were former Optimist sailors. The world had come a long way from 1960s policies that "no young people under 14 years of age can start in any competition" and "a strong policy against children sailing races."

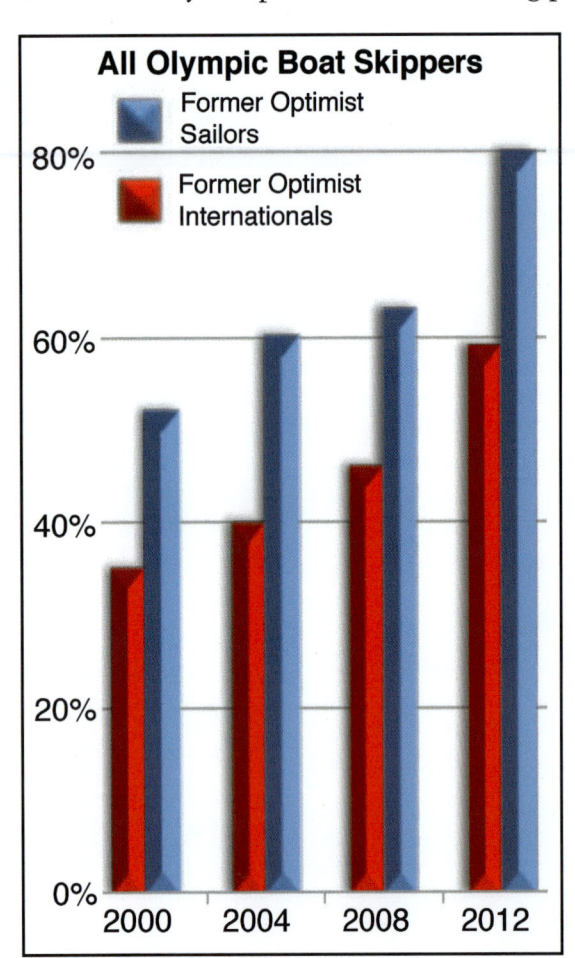
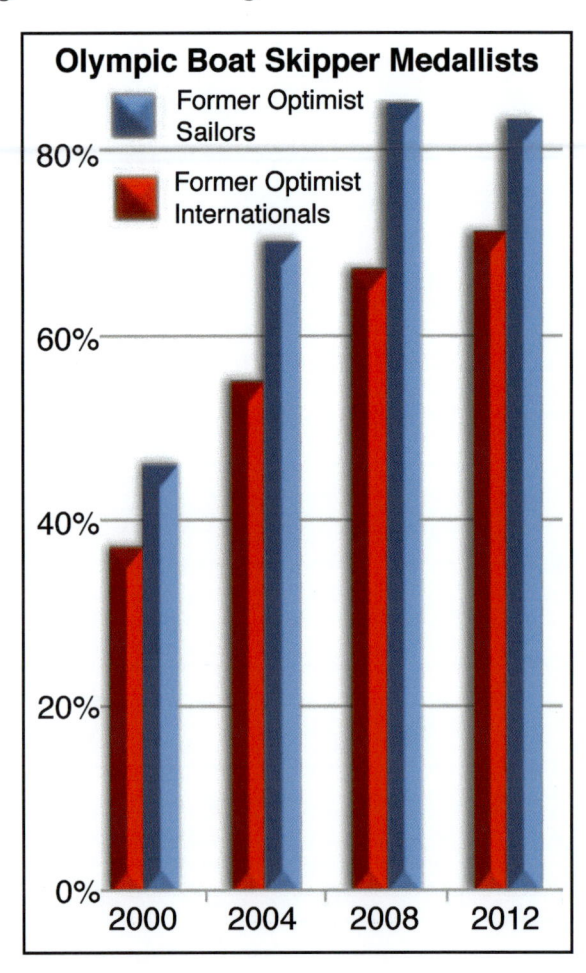

Note: Detailed data at www.wilkessail.net/olympicexops2012.pdf & www.wilkessail.net/lowdropout.pdf

Chapter 13: Summary - the Optimist in 2007

"To co-ordinate youth work between member countries" (IODA Article 2 b)

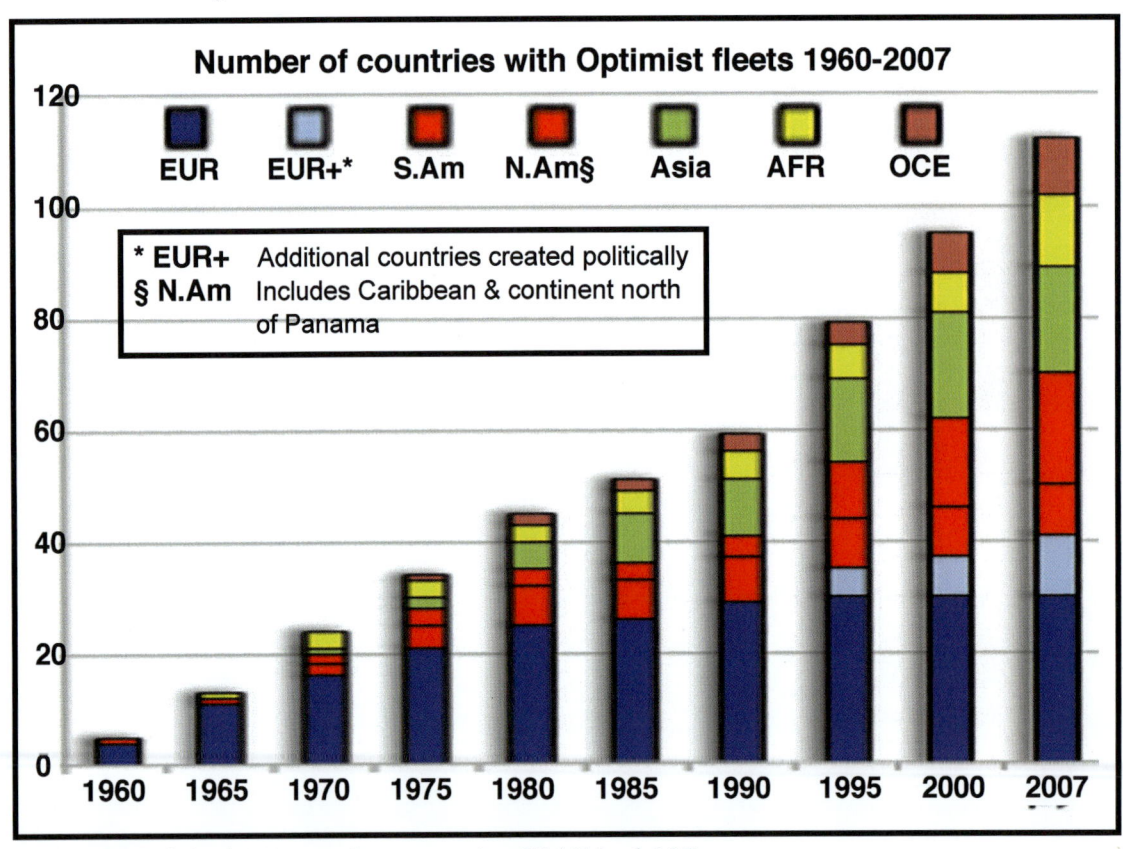

As at 2007 IODA had 111 member countries (ISAF had 125).

"Classes which offer a high standard of international competitive sailing"

(ISAF Regulation 10.1)

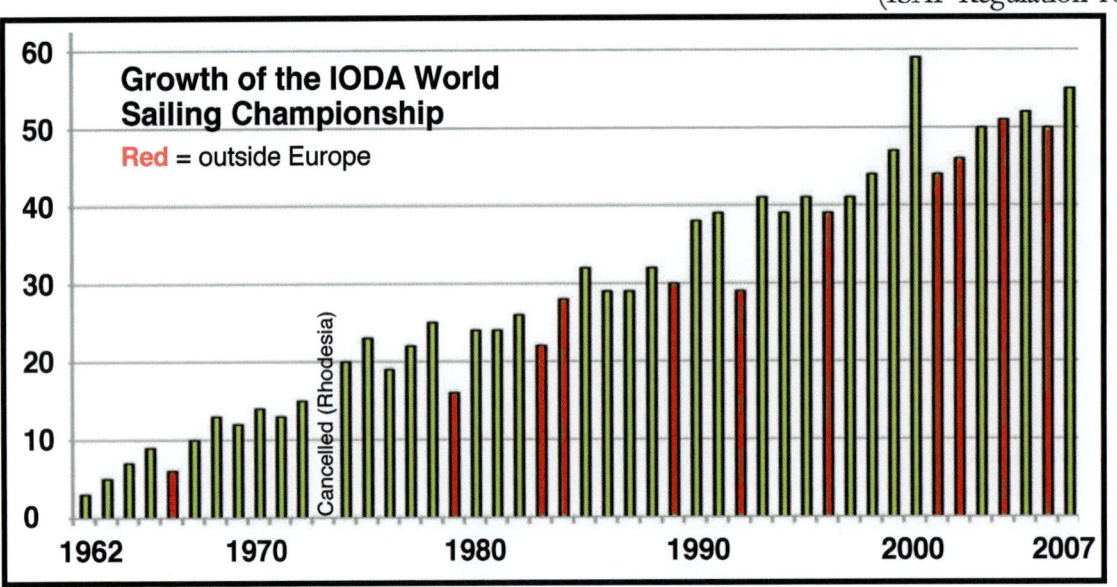

See later in this chapter for participation in continental championships.

"The object of the Class is to provide racing for young people at low cost"

(Class Rule 1.1)

Equipment:

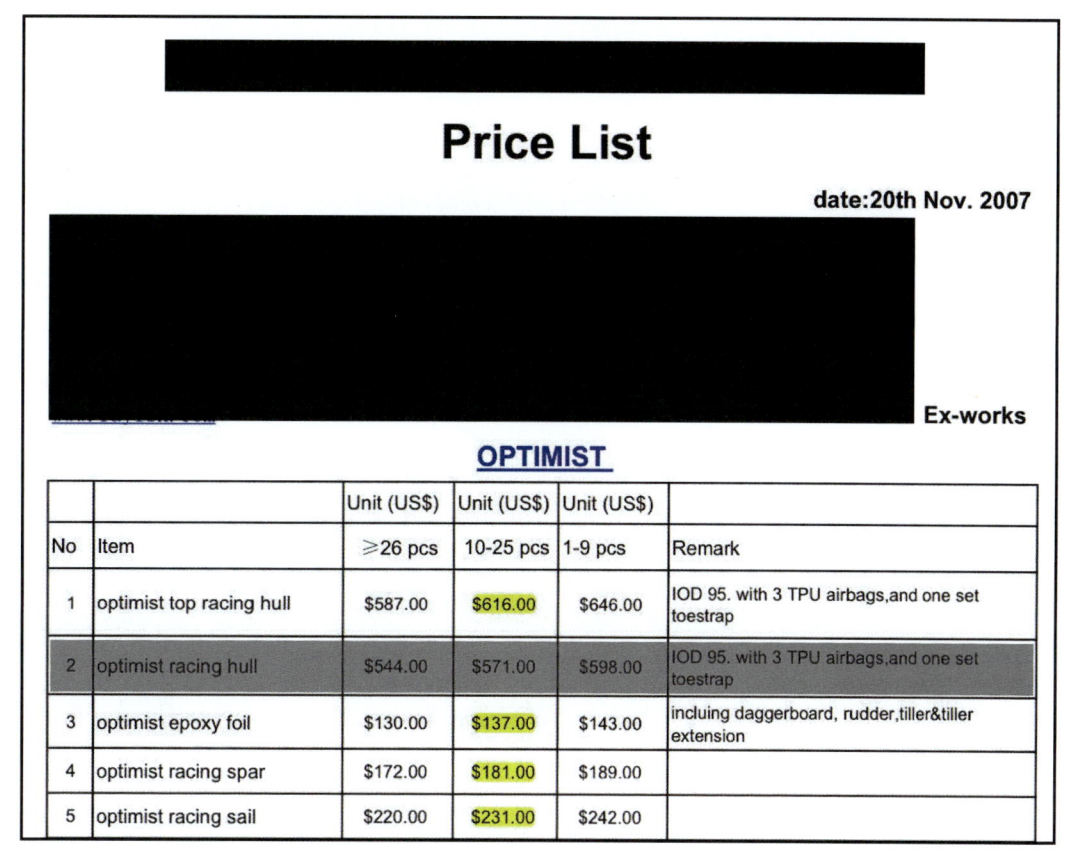

Price List

date:20th Nov. 2007

Ex-works

OPTIMIST

No	Item	Unit (US\$) ≥26 pcs	Unit (US\$) 10-25 pcs	Unit (US\$) 1-9 pcs	Remark
1	optimist top racing hull	\$587.00	\$616.00	\$646.00	IOD 95. with 3 TPU airbags,and one set toestrap
2	optimist racing hull	\$544.00	\$571.00	\$598.00	IOD 95. with 3 TPU airbags,and one set toestrap
3	optimist epoxy foil	\$130.00	\$137.00	\$143.00	incluing daggerboard, rudder,tiller&tiller extension
4	optimist racing spar	\$172.00	\$181.00	\$189.00	
5	optimist racing sail	\$220.00	\$231.00	\$242.00	

Buyers had a choice of 30 builders on four continents.

Events & Charter:

Nine countries from the north and west of Europe chose to charter rather than haul their own boats to Greece. Eight of the top 20 sailors used charter boats.

**I.O.D.A.
EUROPEAN CHAMPIONSHIP 2007**

Varkiza - Athens - Greece

10 - 18 of July 2007

FINAL NOTICE OF RACE

16. ENTRY FEES

16.1. Entry fee including accommodation and meals, between official Arrival Day (July 10th) and Official Departure Day (July 18th) will be per person EUR 480 for sailors and EUR 560 per person for up to three adults.

20. CHARTER BOATS

20.1. Charter boats are **not** mandatory.

20.5. The cost for 8 days (July 10th through July 17th) will be EUR 500. First payment of EUR 200 is due February 7th 2007 and the final payment of EUR 300 is due May 15th 2007. Charter boats will be complete with blocks, air bags, mainsheet, racing spars and racing blades, bailers, paddles, bowlines, everything complying with IODA Class Rules. No sails will be provided. Specific manufacturer and equipment make will be communicated later.

Participation & Supply in 2006/7

The table below, adapted from that published in the 2007 IODA Yearbook, shows participation in the IODA World and continental championship of 2006 & 2007.

The 2006 Worlds had been held in Uruguay and the 2007 in Sardinia. The effect of the policy of developing continental championships (see Chapter 8) is shown by the twenty countries - seven

North America

Country	World	Continental	Either
Antigua			
Bahamas			
Barbados	●		
Bermuda	●	●	
Br. Virgin I.	●	●	
Canada	●	●	
Cuba			
Dominican R.	●	●	
El Salvador			
G. Cayman			
Grenada			
Guatemala	●	●	
Mexico	●	●	
Neth. Antilles	●	●	
Puerto Rico	●	●	
St. Lucia			
St. Vincent			
Trinidad & T.	●	●	
U.S.A.	●	●	●
U.S. Virgin I.	●	●	

South America

Country	World	Continental	Either
Argentina	●	●	●
Brasil	●	●	●
Colombia	●	●	
Chile	●	●	
Ecuador	●	●	
Paraguay	●		
Peru	●	●	
Uruguay	●	●	
Venezuela	●		

Europe

Country	World	Continental	Either
Andorra			
Austria	●	●	
Belarus			
Belgium	●	●	
Bulgaria		●	
Croatia	●	●	
Cyprus		●	
Czech Rep.	●	●	●
Denmark	●	●	●
Estonia		●	
Finland	●	●	●
France	●	●	●
Germany	●	●	
Georgia			
Great Britain	●	●	●
Greece	●	●	●
Hungary	●	●	●
Iceland			
Ireland	●	●	●
Israel	●	●	
Italy	●	●	●
Latvia	●		
Lithuania		●	
Macedonia FYR			
Malta			
Monaco		●	

KEY:

●	Attended 2006 or 2007 IODA World Championship	62
●	Attended 2006 or 2007 IODA Continental Championship	77
	Attended either	83

Asian, six African, four European and three Oceanian - choosing to participate in continentals rather than Worlds.

There were 30 builders in 23 countries on four continents, buying in total over 4,000 plaques a year.

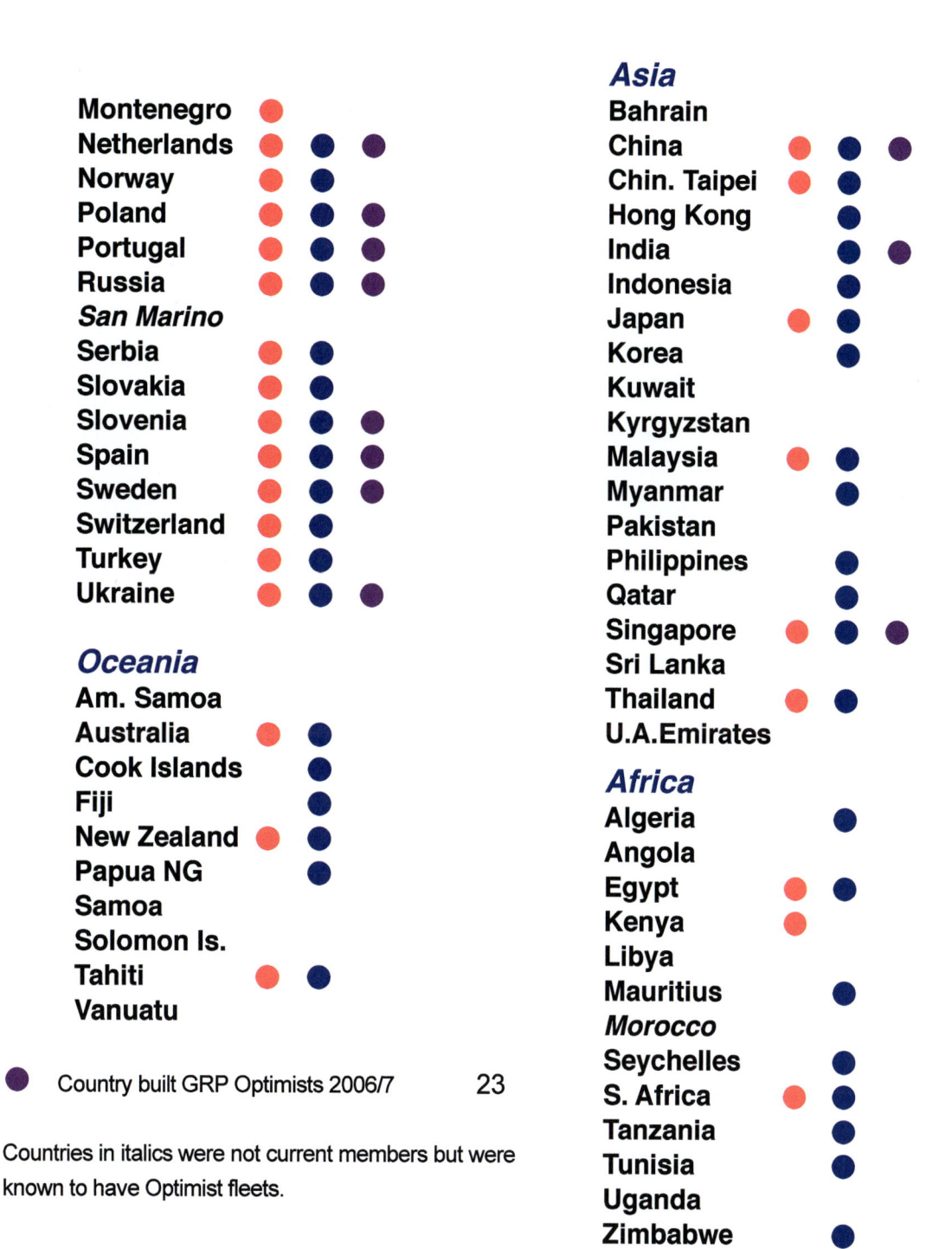

Montenegro
Netherlands
Norway
Poland
Portugal
Russia
San Marino
Serbia
Slovakia
Slovenia
Spain
Sweden
Switzerland
Turkey
Ukraine

Oceania
Am. Samoa
Australia
Cook Islands
Fiji
New Zealand
Papua NG
Samoa
Solomon Is.
Tahiti
Vanuatu

Country built GRP Optimists 2006/7   23

Countries in italics were not current members but were known to have Optimist fleets.

Asia
Bahrain
China
Chin. Taipei
Hong Kong
India
Indonesia
Japan
Korea
Kuwait
Kyrgyzstan
Malaysia
Myanmar
Pakistan
Philippines
Qatar
Singapore
Sri Lanka
Thailand
U.A.Emirates

Africa
Algeria
Angola
Egypt
Kenya
Libya
Mauritius
Morocco
Seychelles
S. Africa
Tanzania
Tunisia
Uganda
Zimbabwe

Appendix: Executive Committee Members 1962-2007

Presidents

Viggo Jacobsen (DEN)	1962-1981
Nigel Ringrose (GBR)	1981-1985
Al Chandler (THA)	1985-1989
Helen Mary Wilkes (IRL)	1989-1998
René Kluin (NED)	1998-2006
Peter Barclay (PER)	2006-*2007*

Secretaries:

Edith Jacobsen (DEN)	1962-1981
Hanne Rix (DEN)	1981-1997
Robert Wilkes (IRL)	1997-2007

Technical Committee Chairs

Nigel Ringrose (GBR)	
Edmund Spalding (GBR)	1970-1973
Lars Wallin (SWE)	-1981
Eric C. Hansen (DEN)	1981-1984
John Boorman (CAN)	1985-1988
Jens Andersen (DEN)	1988-1990
Patrick Bergmans (BEL)	1991-1992
Dominique Langlois (FRA)	1993-1995
Curly Morris (IRL)	1995-1997
Hans Thijsse (RSA)	1997-2003
Curly Morris (IRL)	2003-*2007*

Regatta Committee Chairs

Al Chandler (THA)	1982-1985
Helen Mary Wilkes (IRL)	1985-1989
Jes Retbøll (DEN)	1989-1991
René Kluin (NED)	1991-1998
Michel Barbier (FRA)	1998-2000
Kenneth Andreasen (USA)	2000-2002
Michel Barbier (FRA)	2002-2004
Luis Ormaechea (ESP)	2004-*2007*

Vice-Presidents

Nigel Ringrose (GBR)
Michel Leduc (FRA)
Lars Wallin (SWE)
Raúl Rivarola (ARG)
Al Chandler (THA)
Jorma Heiskanen (FIN)
Beppy Bruzzone (ITA)
Marc Guichard (FRA)
Helen Mary Wilkes (IRL)
Jes Retbøll (DEN)
Ng Ser Miang (SIN)
Norman Jenkins (ARG)
Gudrun von Dahl (GER)
Maria Santos (POR)
David Booth (RSA)
Hans-Peter Bak (DEN)
Peter Barclay (PER)
José Nigaglioni (PUR)

Treasurers

(other than vice-presidents)
Nigel Ringrose (GBR)
Ivar Ahlgren (SWE)
Aad Offermans (NED)
Roland Tan (MAS)

Presidents of Honour

Viggo Jacobsen (DEN)
Helen Mary Wilkes (IRL)

Members of Honour

Edith Jacobsen (DEN)
Lars Wallin (SWE)
Ivar Ahlgren (SWE)
Nigel Ringrose (GBR)
Eric C. Hansen (DEN)
Al Chandler (THA)
Jens Andersen (DEN)
Beppy Bruzzone (ITA)
Ralph Sjöholm (FIN)
Fred Kats (NED)
Norman Jenkins (ARG)
Robert Wilkes (IRL)
David Booth (RSA)

International Measurers
Eric C. Hansen (DEN)
Dominique Langlois (FRA)
Christoph Meili (BRA)
Takaaki Toda (JPN)
Martin Herman (BEL)
Luis Horta Moragas (ESP)
Curly Morris (IRL)
David Harte (IRL)
Ralph Sjöholm (FIN)
Jean-Luc Gauthier (FRA)
Hyo Kyung Jang (KOR)
Nuno Reis (POR)
Paolo Luciani (ITA)
Wataru Arakawa (JPN)
Diego Freira (URU)

Sources, chapters 4-13

The main sources are the IODA *Optiworlds* and Yearbooks produced by the author.

Other sources include:
IYRU and ISAF Yearbooks
USODA *Optinews*
Jahrbuch der DODV
La Livarde (France)
Optimist Italia
New Zealand Yachting (July 1991)
The "Pope" of Sailing by Paul Franklin Henderson
Close to the Wind by Ben Ainslie
RYA Optimist Handbook by Alan Williams

Online sources including:
Scuttlebutt
Websites of the national Optimist associations

Supplement for Optimist Sailing 1947 - 2007

Clifford McKay Jr.

Introduction

In 1972, I watched the opening ceremony for the Munich Summer Olympics in the harbor at Kiel, Germany, the Yachting venue. As the historic sailing ships from the Age of Sail, paraded stately past, 400 diminutive sails swarmed around them . . . Optis. The contrast was striking . . . the blend of large and small, of old and new, of work and play. The full panorama and history of sail stretched across the harbor, a fitting backdrop for Olympic competition. Excitedly I called my dad to turn on his TV and share the moment. He conceived the idea for the Optimist Pram, and I sailed the first pram on the day it was launched in 1947. We shared many wonderful memories. As we watched the Optis and realized how far Dad's dream had spread, the dream that boys and girls might sail and race, I determined to gather the writings and pictures of those early days and to tell the story of the origin of this little boat.

In the summer of 2012, I anchored my research by reading the microfilm copies of The *Clearwater Sun*, Clearwater's local newspaper. I read the files from March 1947 when the Optimist Club of Clearwater was organized, through August of 1949. Based on the historical data and my first hand experiences, I have written the record of the beginning of Optimist Pram and of the two men who were responsible.

Clark Mills and Major Clifford A McKay developed a boat and a plan to make it affordable so every boy could sail. Thousands of parents and club members all over the world have stepped up to supervise the races, teach safety, transport the young sailors, and provide support. Millions of boys and girls have learned the skills and joys of sailing, as this little boat from the genius of Clark Mills has spread around the world. It all began August 14th, 1947, in Clearwater, Florida, USA

NOTE: Clark Wilbur Mills was known to me as "Clarke", with an "e" sound added to the "Clark." It sounds too formal to call him "Clark," stilted and distant. The best way for me to represent this in writing is to write "Clarke."

CHAPTER i - The Origin of the Optimist Pram

The idea for the Optimist Pram, the forerunner of the Opti Dinghy, was formed at my dining room table. My father, Major Clifford A. McKay, shaped the idea from three components. First, the fun and excitement I had the past 18 months sailing and racing Snipes with the Clearwater Yacht Club Snipe Fleet. He wanted that experience for all boys and girls. Second, my frustration designing and building a Soap Box Derby car, racing it down the hill three times and putting it "out to pasture." He thought a small sailboat could get more use and last longer. Third, the financial structure of the Soap Box Derby in which merchants sponsored the cars and paid the modest costs. Using the Derby model, Dad envisioned a way to pay for the boats so there would be one for every boy who wanted to sail. Instead of work-

ing hard to build a car and ride in it once or twice, each boy with a boat sponsored by a merchant could sail it week after week, learning independence, responsibility, and self confidence.

Major McKay had a unique skill in analyzing a problem, developing a plan, and pulling people together to solve it. He was especially interested in programs for young people. Through the years he had developed creative ways to involve boys and girls in a wide variety of constructive activities. The newly formed Optimist Club invited him to speak and to suggest programs to carry out their motto, "The Friend of the Boy." I was twelve years old at the time and attended that meeting to receive an award as part of the Optimist sponsored Boy Scout Troup.

The *Clearwater Sun* reported on August 15, 1947:

Major Clifford A. McKay, Air Corp Reserves, last night outlined to the Optimist Club a four point program he advocates to help combat the rising tide of juvenile delinquency. Commenting on the Optimist Club's activities in the youth recreation field which include sponsorship of Boy Scout Troup 8 and the staging of the Orange Box Derby, Major McKay suggested: (1) a baseball diamond and playing field on the beach, (2) a Sunday school basketball league, (3) a swimming pool and family recreation center, and (4) a sailboat competition for juniors leading to national competition or regatta in Clearwater. Speaking on the subject: Did You Ever Put Your Hand on the Shoulder of a Red-headed Boy? Major McKay's talk dealt with the importance of parental influence and the home life activities of the boy.

The Optimists liked Dad's idea and asked him to follow up with a boat designer.

The next day Dad called Clark Mills, a local designer and craftsman of small boats. "We need a small sailboat that boys can build. It must cost less than $50, (the same dollar figure used by the Soap Box Derby); it should be built with two sheets of 4' x 8' plywood; and it should use a bed sheet for the sail."

Clarke tells the story this way, Major McKay: *"called me on the phone and asked me to come to his office that evening. He had been a guest speaker at the Optimist Club meeting the night before and said he really had them all fired up ready to pursue a junior sailing program, and he wanted me to draw him a plan for a simple little sailboat that a boy and his dad could build in their garage with simple hand tools. The boat was not to cost over fifty dollars and his idea was to have some merchants and business companies sponsor a kid in return for having the merchant's name on the boat....I was the next couple of nights getting it done. I drew lots of sailboats every night. The problem was the price. Every time I had a nice little sailing skiff drawn, it figured out too much cost. So I finally cut the bow off making it a butt headed pram . . . I finished a sample the following week. I hauled it down to Haven Street Dock in Clearwater and Cliff McKay, Jr. got in and took off in about a 20 mile breeze. He scooted out into the bay on the wind, off the wind, across and then reached back to the dock, he landed saying, 'It was really great!' . . . ."*

I heard this same story told by Dad and by Clarke down through the years. It was always the same, "two sheets of 4 x 8 plywood, a bed sheet for a sail, and cost under $50." Dad was not a sailor. He knew nothing about boat design. He envisioned a small, safe, inexpensive sail boat. His specifics were an attempt to keep the costs down. Clarke said slyly, "I talked him out of the bed sheet," but perhaps a bed sheet subtly suggested to him the shape of the sail in the Sprit Rig so distinctive to the Opti. He said of his "butt headed" pram design that brought the cost under $50, "It looked kinda funny, but it sailed real good."

Clarke continues . . .

"The evening of the next Optimist Club meeting (Sept 4th) which was held in the Grey Moss Inn, I brought the number one pram down and put it right in the entrance foyer all rigged with sail. It caused a flurry of comment by the members as they came in, and they were most all in favor of proceeding with the promotion of the program."

(From *The Writings of Clark Wilbur Mills and Friends*, privately published by Betty McGraw Perkins and David G. Perkins, Jr., 2002).

The *Clearwater Sun* of September 5, 1947 reported:

> Optimist Club members meeting at the Gray Moss Inn last night, heard a program on boats and boat building, presented by Team No. 1 of which Arthur Lee is captain. Guest speakers included Clark Mills, N. M. Faulds, W. Jardine, Commodore Guy Roberts of the Yacht Club, and Major Clifford McKay. Roberts commented on the wider scope of boats and boating and the possibility of a well organized plan to encourage interest in boating in Clearwater. McKay spoke on the originality of design (of the Optimist Pram) and stressed the safety factor.

Dad arranged for persons needed to support the boys building and sailing the boats to attend this meeting…the designer, Clarke Mills; a sailor, Guy Roberts; the Junior High School Wood Shop Instructor, Willard Jardine; and N. M. Faulds, principal of the Junior High School who had incorporated several Industrial Arts programs in his school.

The Sun, Clearwater, Florida, Friday, September 5, 1947

OPTIMISTS HEAR BOAT PROGRAM

Optimist Club members, meeting at the Gray Moss Inn last night, heard a program on boats and boat building, presented by Team No. 1 of which Arthur Lee is captain.

Guest speakers included Clark Mills, N. M. Faulds, W. Jardine, Commodore Guy Roberts of the Yacht Club and Maj. Clifford McKay.

Roberts commented on the wider scope of boats and boating and the possibility of a well organized plan to encourage interest in boating in Clearwater. McKay spoke on the originality of design and stressed the safety factor.

Roberts, Robert Wilfong and Dick Moore were guests of Maynard Bayney; Daniel Barker was the guest of Jim Robison; W. Moore was the guest of Arthur Lee; R. Blossom the guest of Daniel Gogston; while Faulds, Jardine, McKay and Mills were program guests.

Jardine and Faulds were ready to assist the boys building their boats.

This rather brief report of the meeting was elaborated by the *Clearwater Sun* two days later in its Sunday Edition:

The Clearwater Optimist Club last night announced as its latest project the sponsorship of the building of a fleet of "pram" boats for boys, and the staging of a pram regatta in the bay here, to be followed possibly by a state and national competition.

The pram is a single-masted sailboat, seven feet, two inches long [sic], 42 inches beam, with a blunt nose and with a rake to her keel from abaft the center board well to her forward end.

She is a safe little marine-plywood sailing craft that is original in design, and was created by Clark Mills of Clearwater . . .

Local merchants and individuals are to sponsor prams, retaining title subject to rules and regulations of the Optimist Club Pram Committee, composed of W. Watson, chairman, Art Lee, Ben Magrew and Maynard Barney.

The overall cost of the pram is estimated at about $50 or less. Plans, specifications and construction procedures are completely detailed by printed instructions, pictures and blueprints available to boys through their sponsors.

Boys from 10 to 16 years of age are to be selected to build their own boats from applicants who qualify for ability to do the job, selection to be made by a committee consisting of N. M. Faulds, Principal, Clearwater Junior High School, W. Jardine, head of manual training department, Clearwater Junior High and Optimist Clark Mills. Prams will be built at the boys' homes or at places provided by the sponsors.

Commodore Guy Roberts of the Clearwater Yacht Club and the seasoned sailors of that organization have prepared rules and regulations covering use of the prams. The pram

---

The Sun, Clearwater, Florida, Sunday, September 7, 1947

Optimists Sponsor 'Pram' Fleet, Regatta, for Boys

The Clearwater Optimist Club last night announced as its latest project the sponsorship of the building of a fleet of "pram" boats for boys, and the staging of a pram regatta in the bay here, to be followed possibly by a state and national competition.

The pram is a single-masted sailboat, seven feet, two inches long, 42 inches beam, with a blunt nose and with a rake on her keel from abaft the center board well to her forward end.

She is a safe little marine-plywood sailing craft that is original in design, and was created by Clark Mills of Clearwater and the Prior Boat Works in Dunedin.

Local merchants and individuals are to sponsor prams, retaining title subject to rules and regulations of the Optimist Club Pram Committee, composed of W. Watson, chairman, Art Lee, Ben Magrew and Maynard Barney.

The overall cost of the pram is estimated at about $50 or less. Plans, specifications and construction procedure is completely detailed by printed instructions, pictures and blueprints available to boys through their sponsors.

Boys from 10 to 16 years of age are to be selected to build their own boats from applicants who qualify for ability to do the job, selection to be made by a committee consisting of N. M. Faulds, principal, Clearwater Junior High School, W. Jardine, head of manual training department, Clearwater Junior and Senior High Schools and Optimist Clark Mills. Prams will be built at the boys' homes or at places provided by the sponsors.

Commodore Guy Roberts of the Clearwater Yacht Club and the seasoned sailors of that organization have prepared rules and regulations covering use of the prams. The pram fleet will be divided into classes, the first being the novice class into which all the boys starting to sail will fall. As they improve in proficiency they stand for promotion from a holder of novice class papers up to the rating of senior mariner.

An annual regatta will be held in Clearwater Bay to select the national champion pram sailor. Plans are so set-up and copyrighted that use of the name, design of boat, title to and use of craft, etc., is governed by the Optimist Club of Clearwater.

The first Optimist pram already built, is to be sailed in the Yacht Club basin this afternoon. Boys and sponsors interested are invited, as well as the public. Next week the pram will be on display in the windows of the Florida Power Corp., Cleveland Street. Fifteen sponsors have been obtained and the Optimist Pram Committee expects a fleet of not less than 50 to be ready for the first full-scale regatta some time in the spring.

> fleet will be divided into classes, the first being the novice class into which all the boys starting to sail will fall. As they improve in proficiency they stand for promotion from a holder of novice class papers up to the rating of senior mariner.
>
> An annual regatta will be held in Clearwater Bay to select the national champion pram sailor. Plans are so set-up and copy-righted that use of the name, design of boat, title to and use of craft, etc. is governed by the Optimist Club of Clearwater.
>
> The first Optimist pram already built is to be sailed in the Yacht Club basin this afternoon. Boys and sponsors interested are invited, as well as the public. Next week, the pram will be on display in the windows of the Florida Power Corp., Cleveland Street. Fifteen sponsors have been obtained and the Optimist Pram Committee expects a fleet of not less than 50 to be ready for the first full-scale regatta sometime in the spring.

The article outlines Major McKay's plan in detail. Since he began work as a newspaper reporter, dad often wrote the story himself and offered it to the newspaper, saving them time and effort and helping assure accuracy. Dad's dreams were always large. From the first, he expected a State and a National regatta. In December of 1948, the first large regatta was further inflated to an International Regatta, in spite of the fact that the competitors came from the nearby towns of Dunedin, Pass-a-Grill, and St. Petersburg, the farthest, only 25 miles away.

Clarke and the Optimist Club worked hard to keep the cost at $50. Merchants came forward as sponsors. Fifteen signed up the first week, including many Optimist Club Members. Clarke began building prams, and on November 16th, 1947, a fleet of eight raced off the Yacht Club Basin on Clearwater Bay.

Clark Mills said in a letter to my sister in 1996, after our father's death, "I firmly believe that Major McKay was the main instigator of the very successful Optimist Pram Program....I'm sure it was just as everyone said, a block-buster of a talk that started the Pram program."

Dad's creative imagination and persuasiveness, Clark Mills design genius and boat building skills, and the Optimist Club's energy and enthusiasm originated and launched the Optimist Pram.

NOTE 1: The language was about "Boys,"... .which was typical of the times. The Optimist Motto was "The Friend of the Boy." But the reality was on March 4th, 1948, only 6 months later, The Clearwater Optimist Club voted to include girls in the Pram program. Susan Smith was welcomed to the Clearwater Fleet, sailing the Palm Pavilion pram. The nearby Dunedin Fleet, organized in May, had girl skippers from the beginning, Carol and Jackie Longstreet, Allison Delaney and Barbara Skinner.

Did girls sail in skirts?!

CHAPTER ii - "I sailed the first Optimist Pram"

My dad, Major Clifford McKay suggested to the Optimist Club, a plan that would provide a small sailboat funded by merchants for boys to sail and race, similar to the little cars of the Soap Box Derby. He thought why not race small boats instead of cars? Florida is short on hills, but long on water. They could sail all year long on Clearwater Bay. The Optimist Club liked the idea and before the meeting adjourned asked Major McKay to follow up.

Dad met with Clark Mills the next night and suggested a few criteria designed to help hold the cost to $50. In less than a week, Clarke conceived and designed the Optimist Pram. He built a prototype, painted it red, and brought it to the Haven Street Dock for a sail. He sailed it briefly and, satisfied with its performance, he turned it over to me. It was lively and accelerated smartly as the sail filled. It turned sharply when I put the tiller over. The bow didn't dig in. It seemed to lift and skip across the water. The low sprit rig and generous beam gave it good stability. It was fun and easy to sail. I thought, "Wow, this is neat." The Snipe I'd been sailing was a little big for me, but the Pram felt just right.

Clarke built a jig to hold the transom, the bow, and a mid-ship thwart. He joined them together with narrow cypress stringers. He glued and nailed quarter inch plywood over the frame. Clarke said, "I hammered it together in a day and a half with ridged nails, slapped on a coat of paint and called her an Optimist Pram."

Dad's original plan, following the Soap Box Derby, was that the boys and their fathers would build the boats. However, we boys never built the hull, nor did we attempt to design it like we did our Soap Box Derby cars. Amateur designs aren't feasible for boats, and even Clarke's straight forward design wasn't easy for amateur builders. I know, I built four Prams with my son in 1973. The change from each boy building his own boat was never discussed. It was obvious to all. Clarke built the

hulls. We boys took it from there, fastening the corner caps, installing the bow thwart and mast step, scraping off the glue that dripped down, sanding, painting, shaping the rudder and dagger board edges, bending the rudder fittings from galvanized sheet metal in the vice at the school woodworking shop, and tying the sail to the mast with venetian blind cord from the hardware store. Dickie Moore, a local sail maker, built the sails from common duck cloth. The mast was a 1 ½" dowel from the lumber yard. At first, the sheet ran from the boom, through a block on the top of the tiller. You could hold the tiller and sheet in one hand. There was no cleat, no traveler. These came later. When you mounted the rudder fittings on the boat and on the rudder, you had to make sure to get it right, or the sheet would lift the rudder up and off. The fittings on the rudder must go inside the two on the transom. Failing to mount them correctly could produced some exciting moments as the rudder lifted up and the boat sailed off with no means to steer it. Sponsors painted their names on the boats. My sponsor was WTAN, the local radio station. Sometimes the newspaper when reporting a race, would list the winners by the sponsor's name rather than by the skipper.

not a good idea!

NOTE: There was no flotation. The Pram was made of wood. It would float, well enough to support both itself and the skipper. There were also no Personal Flotation Devices. The only PFDs at that time were ones with a canvas vest that held blocks of cork, bulky and cumbersome to wear and used mostly for an emergency on commercial ships. The Navy during WW II developed a nylon vest with plastic bags enclosing kapok fiber, but they were not commonly available. Besides, Clearwater Bay was shallow, and the water was warm. All of us boys grew up spending almost as much time in the water as we did on the land. The Gulf and the Bay were like a second home to us. We also lacked gloves, wet suits and other technical clothing. We sailed in a bathing suit and a T shirt. Life was......well....simpler.

The Optimist committee held races every Sunday afternoon, off the end of Baymont Street near the Old Fish House where the prams were stored. It was a steep learning curve for the committee and boys alike, but everyone had fun. Sunday afternoons we'd race, but after school and on Saturdays, we'd help each other carry the boats to the water and make sail. We explored Clearwater Bay and its mangrove islands on our own. The only rule was "Do not sail in the Gulf." The warm, shallow waters of the bay were protective of the small boats and their skippers. Of course, even while exploring, we were honing our racing skills . . . when two or more boats sail together, it's a race.

In addition to sailing skills, I learned that the wind dies in the late afternoon, and it's a long paddle home. I learned to sail in 6" of water over the shallow grass flats by heeling to lift the rudder almost entirely out of the water. I discovered that my pram would stand up nicely in 30 knots of wind. The only problem was bailing out the spray that splashed in. One hot day, between races, I capsized, to cool off with a brief swim. I pulled the boat up on the beach, dumped out the water, and returned in time for the next start. I won handily. Before the subsequent race, two others capsized. The three of us outdistanced the field with ease. The wet sail kept air from passing through the duck cloth and created a better airfoil. We learned by experimenting. (Sorry guys, your modern Dacron sails are already air tight so this trick won't work now-a-days.) I never capsized a pram by accident. It was always on purpose.

The boys from Dunedin heard us talking at school and saw to it that they got some Prams. The Florida Sailing Association approved the Optimist Pram for their sponsored races in April of '49. Ernie Green, now head of the Optimist Committee, offered his moving van to transport the fleet to

Florida Sailing Association Regattas. The Prams created quite a stir when the huge Green Moving and Storage Van pulled up at the launch site and disgorged boat after boat onto Sarasota Bay. Older sailors marveled at these little "water bugs" scooting around. My uncle, a seasoned sailor, jokingly offered me his shoe lace to replace the line that held my sail to the mast. The humor and disdain of veteran sailors quickly turned to respect when they saw the skill and the passion of the young skippers. The Prams drew attention wherever they sailed. Optimist Clubs in surrounding cities sponsored fleets. Yacht Clubs from around Florida adopted them. Winter visitors saw the Optimist Prams and took the plans north with them.

By 1948 medals were given for weekly races. Scores were totaled each month and a trophy awarded for the best score. In December the first "International Pram Regatta" was held with Peter Duvoisin taking first place. Pete and I lived next door to each other and were good friends. We both loved to sail and often found ourselves in close competition. We were tied going into the last race. We took turns leading for the first five legs. On the entire last leg, a broad reach with a slight swell coming in from the pass from the Gulf, we were so close we could have reached across and shaken hands. He'd catch a wave and surge forward. Then I'd catch one. He caught the last one and beat me by 18". It was good competition and great fun. Boats came from Clearwater, Dunedin, Pass-a-Grille, and St. Petersburg. It was hardly international but the dreams and expectations for the Optimist Pram were always large, as large as the boat was small.

Pete

"The pram shed's on fire," Dad said, as he shook me awake about midnight, April 20th, 1949. I was pulling on my pants and jacket as I ran to the car. "Can't you drive any faster?" I urged, as we drove in silence the half mile down the beach. The night sky glowed like daylight as the orange flames leapt into the air. The Old Fish House, built during the Great Depression by government paid workers housed a Sea Scout Troup, the Power Squadron, and the Pram Fleet. Its roof was sheet metal as were its sides. The floor and rafters were wooden beams, dry tinder ready to burn. When we arrived, the entire building was totally engaged. Nothing inside could be saved. The Pram fleet was going up in flames.

We did what we could. We helped cast boats loose from nearby Yacht Club slips and pushed them away from harm. We pulled racing Snipes on trailers out of a shed close to the inferno, some with completely flat tires. Then, as the firemen were beginning to tire after hours of strain, we helped hold the powerful fire hoses. By dawn, the Fish House was reduced to smoldering embers and the ashes of 29 prams. The only ones saved were a few that boys had taken home for a repair or to touch up the paint.

At school the next day, it was hard to think of anything other than the fire. The fun and excitement of last year and a half vanished overnight, consumed by the flames. When the ashes cooled a few days later, I poked around for metal fittings from my boat. All I found were melted blobs.

Possibly the first ever Optimist race.
Sail numbers had not yet been allocated, nor had the sponsors' decals been applied.

The sailboat *Salty* belonged to the sail maker Dickie Moore, and the power committee boat with the flag to Wallis Skinner, the first fleet captain.

Dad, the General Manager of WTAN, the local radio station, called news commentator Howard Hartley. Mr. Hartley went on the air, told the story of the fire, and of the dismayed heart-broken youngsters. He asked listeners to sponsor boats to rebuild the fleet. The phones began to ring and in less than two hours generous merchants and friends contributed funds for 43 new boats to replace the 29 lost. In addition, they donated $6,000 in building materials for a new shed. I was at the radio station that night and helped answer the phones.

Clarke burned the midnight oil building new boats. The story of the community's generosity spread, carrying with it the story of the amazing Optimist Pram and the boys and girls that sailed them. The fire became a springboard that launched the Pram on its worldwide journey.

For me, sailing an Optimist Pram was the start of a life time sailing, racing, and cruising. It was the beginning of "a lifelong apprenticeship" in the finest sport there is. Everywhere I go there are Optis. I've sailed past Coconut Grove, Florida, the western horizon white with Pram sails. I was awakened in Marion, Massachusetts to the squeals of Pram sailors practicing capsizing. I rescued a beginning skipper who'd been blown away from her race at Nantucket, Massachusetts. I've watched prams race in Interlaken, Switzerland and Oxford, Maryland. I've seen the Prams stowed on the quay in Funchal in the Madeira Islands and in Copenhagen, Denmark. And then there was the TV coverage of the Opening Ceremonies in Kiel Germany, the yachting venue of the Munich Olympics as the fleet of 400 Optis, dwarfed by the Tall Ships, swarmed among them claiming their place as sailors among sailors in these rich historic traditions.

The beginning of the Optimist Pram was a labor of love. Dad conceived a plan so all kids could sail and promoted the Pram around the state. In seven years there were more than a thousand of them racing in Florida alone. Clark Mills designed it, built many of the first hulls, and donated the copyright to the Clearwater Optimist Club. The Clearwater Optimist Club with Ernie Green's tireless leadership spent countless hours with the program, supervising races, working with the boys and girls, and transporting them to regattas. The Optimists practiced their motto, "The Friend of the Boy." No one received royalties or any remuneration. Dad's plan worked. It provided inexpensive boats sponsored by merchants for every boy to spend hours and hours on the water, with no time to think about getting into trouble. The goal of these men was that boys and girls could have fun sailing, and grow up to be good citizens . . . and that alone was their reward.

Clarke's skills could have built anything he chose, but he explained his passion for boats, a passion that breathes through every fiber of his Optimist Pram: "A house is a house. But a boat, it's just a gleamin' beautiful creation. And when you pull the sail up on a boat, you've got a little bit of something God-given. Man, it goes bleatin' off like a bird wing, you know, and there's nothing else like it."

Millions of boys and girls on six continents have "flown on those bird wings" in Clarke's amazing little boat, and it has changed their lives.

. . . grow up to be good citizens. The first generation of Optimist graduates. Cliff seated at right.

CHAPTER iii: Program Rules & Regulations

BY-LAWS

Section 1. RACING SEASON. The official racing season may extend a full 12 months from August 1st to July 31st.

Section 2. MEASUREMENTS. All measurements of the Optimist Class Pram, the sails, and the mast, must be in agreement with the official plans which are obtainable from the parent organization only, and are not transferrable. Any pram not complying with the official measurements shall not be eligible for registration or participation in any sanctioned regatta.

Section 3. RULES. Except where contrary to rules or restrictions of the Optimist Class Pram, the rules of the North American Yacht Racing Union shall govern all races.

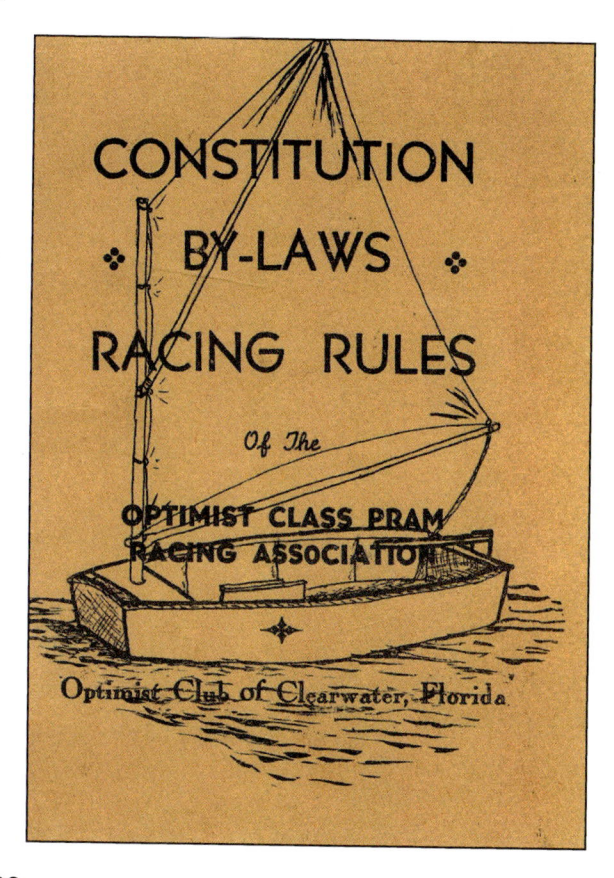

CONSTITUTION

❖ BY-LAWS ❖

RACING RULES

Of The

OPTIMIST CLASS PRAM RACING ASSOCIATION

Optimist Club of Clearwater, Florida

RULES AND REGULATIONS FOR THE CLEARWATER OPTIMIST PRAM SKIPPERS

1. In order to be assigned a pram, the skipper or his parents must fill out and sign the Optimist Pram International Racing Association application. (This application is available at the pram shed.) A fee of one dollar must accompany the application. The application will then be filed in the order received. As prams become available the boy or girl whose name appears on the top application, will be notified by word, if present at the pram shed, or in writing, if not present. After written notice is sent out the skipper will have one week to claim the boat unless sickness requires additional time. If not claimed, the next person in order will be so notified.

2. The skipper must be able to swim.

3. The age range is from the skippers ninth (9) birthday to his fifteenth (15) birthday.

4. No pram is to be removed from the pram shed at anytime without the permission of a member of the Boy's Work Committee. (This means for the purpose of repairs, painting or sundry reasons.)

5. No skipper is permitted to sail his pram unless accompanied by another pram or boat. You are not permitted to take your pram out alone.

6. The pram must be sailed in the bay adjacent to or in the near vicinity of the pram shed. Unless directed otherwise by the Boy's Work Committee.

7. It is the responsibility of each skipper to maintain his or her pram and keep it in good order. This includes such things as painting when necessary, keeping the sail, mast, rudder, tiller and center board in good condition. If on inspection by any member of the Boys Work Committee any of the above things are neglected, and the skipper is notified of this neglect, doesnot within a reasonable time make the necessary repairs, the boat will be assigned to another skipper.

8. Official races will be held at 2 PM on the first and third Sunday's of each month, when the weather is suitable. The second and fourth Sunday's will be used for any postponed races.

9. Skippers must sail each sunday when official races are scheduled. If two Sunday's of official sailings are missed without some ligitimate sxcuse the skipper will forfeit his pram and the pram will be reassigned. Some member of the Boy's Work Committee must be notified, preferably previous to races, of any excuseable absence. The Boy's Work Committee will judge the legitimacy of the excuse.

10. It will be the responsibility of the skippers to keep the pram shed in order. After each sunday of racing three skippers will be assigned to do this. Every skipper will be assigned in his or her turn.

11. The fee is one dollar each year and is collected about July 1st. If a skipper joins the fleet after   July 1st the fee will be prorated on a quarterly basic. (This fee is to be earned by the skipper.)

12. If a skipper purchases a sail, rudder, mast, tiller, center board or any other accessories for the repair of his or her pram such will become the property of the Optimist Club, when the skipper relinquishes his or her pram.

13. Skippers the pram is not yours. It is assigned to you, to sail and use but not to ABUSE.

YOUR BOY'S WORK COMMITTEE

General Charimen

Howard Smith

Recorder

Tom Graham

Committee No.1. (Jan,Mar,May,Jul,Sep,Nov,)

    Ernie Green   Chariman
    Dick Drossler
    Joe York
    Howard Smith

Committee No. 2 (Feb,Apr,Jun,Aug,Oct,Dec,)

    Duane Crawmer   Chairmen
    Chich Phillips
    Fred Walbolt
    Bill Chauncey

Yes, they were watching!

Pram Racing Rules

Adapted from the then current racing rules of the North American Yacht Racing Union

4. TOUCHING A MARK - A pram shall not touch a mark unless wrongfully forced to do so by another pram, in which case she must protest.

CHAPTER iv Clarke Mills, the Designer of the Optimist Pram

The designer of the Optimist Pram, Clark Wilbur Mills moved to Clearwater, Florida, from Jackson, Michigan, when he was 3 years old. World War I had just ended. His father sold his grocery store which provided the cash needed to make the move south. His dad was clever and creative, a good model for a son who would become a designer and builder. He worked with his hands and could fix anything that needed fixing, and he could build most anything he wanted. He took his young son and his skills to Florida and started life there. Clarke's grandfather was a cabinet maker, and in addition to cabinets and furniture, he built a wealth of small wooden pieces just for fun during the long winter nights in Michigan. His father and grandfather were good models and teachers and provided Clarke a love of building, extensive wood working skills, and great confidence.

As a toddler, Clarke found a bag of nails and a hammer in the house, so he drove all the nails into the living room floor. His mother was furious, but dad saw it differently, he admired how skillfully he had driven the nails. As a boy, Clearwater Bay captured Clarke's imagination. He built boats using sheet metal on a wooden frame and sealed the seams with tar. But sheet metal boats were hard to move through the water. So he stretched canvas over a wooden frame and painted it. It worked like a kayak and was much easier to move . . . but it still had to be paddled. Finally, he designed and built a small sailboat to sail across the bay's sparkling waters, let the sails do the work . . . he no longer had to paddle. He liked sailing. He liked it so much that he built other sail boats for himself and for his friends. Together they organized the Clearwater Junior Yacht Club at the Haven Street Dock and sailed on Clearwater Bay.

When the clouds of war darkened in 1939, Clarke was a young man looking for work. He worked in housing construction and applied for a government boatbuilding job. But when the Japanese attacked Pearl Harbor, he decided to join the Navy. Just before he'd signed up for the Navy, however, his application to work in the Philadelphia Navy Yard in the Small Boat Shop was approved, so feeling he could serve better there, he moved north to Philadelphia.

The Boat Shop was a block long with a crew of 130. "It's not like I was intimidated, " said Clarke, "I was scared spitless. The shop superintendent asked me what kind of boats I built. I pulled my wallet out and showed him a little snapshot of the sloop Richard and I had built, and he said without hesitating, "You will start here as boatbuilder 3rd class." I guess I was just pretty up tight. I said I hadn't come all this way for no 3rd class! No sir I am a first class boat builder and to hell with it.

The superintendent calmed him down, explaining that if he was good, he'd make second and first class in no time, and persuaded him to give it a try. The Small Boat Shop extended his knowledge of boats. He learned quickly and proved his skill. He was soon promoted to first class builder, the first in his group to achieve this honor. In a few weeks he was transferred to the Big Boat Shop and taught how to make the stems for the Navy's 50' Motor Launches. He was always good friends with his fellow workers. They shared knowledge and skills with one another and enjoyed one another's company.

In the middle of World War II, Clarke had had enough of cold weather, so he packed his tools, left Philadelphia, and moved to the Panama Canal Zone as a shipwright. He faced new challenges, but he continued to increase his building skills and gather new friends around him. The tropical waters were most inviting, so in his spare time he designed and built an 18' sailboat from scraps in order to sail the waters of the Canal Zone. Designing and building sailboats was his hobby, his life's work and his passion.

When the war ended, he returned to Clearwater to see if he could make a living designing and building boats. Whether or not he was a 3rd class builder when he started in Philadelphia, by the time he opened his Boat Works in Dunedin with his friend Walter Pryor, with all he had learned and with his developed skills and experience, he was now clearly First Class.

I met Clarke in 1946 when I first discovered sailing with the Clearwater Snipe Fleet. I was eleven.

I'd get off the school bus, walk across the Clearwater Yacht Club grounds to the old Fish House shed, a cavernous tin building, where in the dark back corner Clark Mills was building a 24' sailboat. A little light crept in through the old weathered windows, but the main light was from two small naked bulbs hung over the work. Clarke always had time for an eleven year old boy. He liked visiting as he worked. He could maintain a lively conversation while his hands deftly crafted the next piece for the boat. He loved wood, all kinds of wood, but especially ordinary woods like pine, oak, cypress and fir. He understood wood, and it responded to his touch. The result was always smooth curves and tight fitting joints. We talked about sailing and boats, we talked about building boats, we talked about Florida and how it had changed since he first arrived in the 1920s. He was friendly and gregarious. He loved people, he loved life, and he loved to build boats.

Around us in the Old Fish House were racing Snipes resting on their trailers. Clarke didn't race much, but he had repaired many of these boats for his friends. When he built a couple of racing Snipes for local men, the boats sailed so well and won so many races that he soon had orders from all over the United States, orders that would take him much more than a year to fill. At that point, he started returning their deposits. He had too much work to do. A few years before when he first opened his shop he was concerned about enough work. Now he had more than he could handle.

I asked him about "Mills Snipes." Had they a flatter keel with less rocker? Did he build them fuller in the bow? What made them sail fast? In his usual modest manner he answered, "Shucks, I just try to get them inside the narrow tolerances of class measurements. I'm just glad if they 'measure in'." Those who raced them knew better.

He learned from his family to work hard, but also to take time to play. He described gunk-holing in a sailboat as "sailing down the coast, and when you see someone, or something on shore that interests you, you drop the anchor and go ashore and spend a few days." He had a great sense of humor and loved to laugh. He proposed the first movable ballast for a sailboat. "You load the bilge with turtles. When you tack, they'll crawl up to the high side."

When it came to the Optimist Pram, he designed it quickly, drawing on ideas for small boats that constantly rolled around in his head. It was hard to design a boat for under $50, but he kept working at it . . . and succeeded. He always seemed a little surprised at the little boat and its popularity, and a little embarrassed at the attention he received. When his grandson asked him why he was famous, he explained that people like his little boat that looked like a "horse trough". He told the story of a man asking him to build him a Pram with the stringers and keel on the outside. As Clarke was explaining that it wouldn't sail well and wouldn't be stable, the man commented that he thought it would be a great place to mix concrete. Clarke was a self-deprecating genius, well liked, fun to be around who was grateful to make a modest living doing what he loved, building and designing boats.

Dad's original idea was for the boys to build their own boats, but that never happened. Unlike the Soap Box Derby Cars that only needed to be mechanically sound and have similar wheels to be competitive, boats needed to be same hull, same sails and same weight to be fair for all. The skill level to build the boats was beyond the boys and many of their fathers. As the demand grew, Clarke would cut out pieces for 12 or more boats. He'd mount the transom, bow and midship thwart on a heavy jig. The jig held them strong and true as he screwed on the stringers and keel, mounted the dagger board well, and then attached the plywood with ridged bronze nails and casein glue. The sturdy wooden boats never leaked, and stood up to the rough treatment of a bunch of boys.

When Prams and Optis were built with fiberglass and interest in wooden prams was waning, Clarke designed and built several large power boats including a double hulled fishing boat for daily charter in the Gulf. He said, "I wasn't sure about the double hull, so I got some Styrofoam, shaped a scale model and pulled it through the water to see how it worked. It must have worked okay since that boat has been out in all sorts of weather for years now."

Clark Mills was a soft spoken, unassuming, gregarious, and highly skilled boat designer and builder. He was a master craftsman and warm friend. His fame spread far and wide. My favorite story about him was quoted in *Wooden Boat Magazine*. Two sailing yachts passed in the mid-Atlantic. As is tradition going back to whalers meeting on the high seas, they hailed each other, "Where away?" The west-bound yacht answered. "To Clearwater Florida... .to meet Clark Mills." He was well worth meeting, even if it takes crossing an ocean to do so.

Clark Wilbur Mills is One-of-a-Kind, a capable, unpretentious, and straightforward man, very much like his little boat that has become the largest one-design racing class in the world.

Printed in Great Britain
by Amazon